Judah has written a well-researched and very readable examination of the evidence that supports our faith in God's revelation — the Bible. I strongly encourage anyone who is searching for the truth to read this book.

— GRANT R. JEFFREY, BEST-SELLING AUTHOR AND
INTERNATIONALLY RENOWNED RESEARCHER

Foolish Faith combines a comprehensive scientific accuracy with a good understanding of biblical and philosophical issues, yet it is at the same time clear and comprehensible to the lay reader. Judah takes into account the needs of a reader who may have no familiarity with the Bible or Christianity, giving them additional grounds to trust the Word of God. I believe that this book will encourage many Christians, and will equip them to better understand and defend their faith.

— DR. CARL WIELAND, JOINT CEO,
ANSWERS IN GENESIS MINISTRIES INTERNATIONAL

Foolish Faith proved to be packed with thorough, academically honest investigation. Judah's amalgamation of science and Scripture was so compelling that I invited him to join me on a late-night, open-line television program. I have utmost respect for both the book *Foolish Faith*, and its author.

— RAY DAVID GLENN, HOST AND PRODUCER,
"RISE & SHINE," CTS TELEVISION,
CANADIAN CHRISTIAN TELEVISION

I found *Foolish Faith* to be one of the most interesting and thought-provoking books I have read in a long time. While it is clear that the material in *Foolish Faith* is presenting a certain kind of religious argument and is building toward a particular conclusion, the book is never polemical in the off-putting way that much religious writing can be for non-religious readers like myself. The author's well-articulated and well-documented arguments are not easily dismissed.

— NAOMI GOLD, PH.D. CANDIDATE,
U   S STUDIES

Testimonials

My name is Mark – I'm an apologetics researcher with the Josh McDowell Ministry. I just wanted to commend you on your book, *Foolish Faith*. It's excellent work: readable for laypeople, but it includes the latest apologetics arguments. — MARK, CALIFORNIA

This is just about the greatest book I have seen so far! You've put together some great facts that leave unbelief without excuse. They have also encouraged me and strengthened my faith. The convincingly arranged information in this book has been very useful to me. — AMY, ALABAMA

I stumbled upon your book when one of the pages came up from a web search I was doing on religion. I am a Christian and found your book straightforward, positive, intelligent, and very inspiring. I learned a lot, and it buoyed my faith. I was caught off guard by the title, but the tone of the work kept me interested until I realized what an ingenious title it was. — VICKI

Awesome, awesome book! One of the best Christian apologetics books I've ever read. I'm interested in buying multiple copies for our office Bible study class — and several skeptic friends. Thanks for publishing this wonderful resource. — TOM

This year my interest in religion was sparked again, and my first avenue was to check things out on the Internet. But I found pro-creation websites were so full of "Bible quotes" and sarcasm, and left me with a "believe in Genesis or risk hell" sort of mentality. And the pro-evolution sites read like university biology textbooks and often seemed very dismissive of the Bible, which didn't sit well with me. Then I came across your book and was very impressed with its simple language, extensive backing-up of facts, and reasoning without sarcasm or over-simplified metaphor. I still have questions, but your book was fantastic in clarifying many points for me. It gave me a lot of food for thought, and strengthened my faith. Thank you. — DARRYL

Testimonials edited for brevity and clarity

FOOLISH FAITH

What 21st Century Man Says about God

FOOLISH

FAITH

JUDAH ETINGER

Master
Books

First printing: June 2003

ISBN: 0-89051-399-6
Library of Congress Number: 2003106343

Printed in the United States of America

Please visit our website for other great titles:
www.masterbooks.net

For information regarding author interviews, please contact the publicity department at (870) 438-5288.

CONTENTS

INTRODUCTION

> We go about our daily lives understanding almost
> nothing of the world. Except for children, few of
> us spend much time wondering why nature is the
> way it is; where the [universe] came from, or
> whether it was always here.[1]
>
> — Carl Sagan

Today, almost no one asks whether a particular belief is
true; the question is whether it is "meaningful to me." Thus,
we have a blizzard of conflicting claims. We have moved away
from the belief that everyone has a right to his or her own
opinion, towards the notion that every opinion is equally
"right." Every point of view, since it arises from one's own
feelings, is just as valid as another. Whatever a person feels is
the truth becomes the truth for him or her.[2]

As our calendar continues to move forward, the belief in
one absolute truth becomes less and less important in society.
Thus, an increasingly popular view of God today can be seen
clearly in the words of one journalist:

> For much of my life I was a skeptic. In fact, I con-
> sidered myself an atheist. To me, there was far too
> much evidence that God was merely a product of

wishful thinking, of ancient mythology, of primitive superstition. How could there be a loving God if He consigned people to hell just for not believing in Him? How could miracles contravene the basic laws of nature? Didn't evolution satisfactorily explain how life originated? Doesn't scientific reasoning dispel belief in the supernatural?[3]

— Lee Strobel, former legal
editor of the *Chicago Tribune*

Similarly:

Science involves the study of natural forces only, and ceases to be science when it attempts to explain phenomena by means of supernatural forces.[4]

— American Atheists Website

This quickly growing interpretation of what science is, at the dawn of the new millennium, has made its way from the American Atheists' Website into the mainstream scientific community. But in reality, shouldn't science be a search for the truth, *no matter what the truth might be?*

Many are unaware that today's information age of laptop computers and mobile phones has also revealed sufficient evidence that, surprising as it may be, validates the existence of God. One of the world's most respected cosmologists (who holds the position at Cambridge University once held by Sir Isaac Newton, and who has been hailed by *Time* magazine as "an equal of Einstein") appropriately notes:

I think there are clearly religious implications whenever you start to discuss the origins of the universe. There must be religious overtones. But I think most scientists prefer to shy away from the religious side

of it. . . . The odds against a universe that has produced life like ours are immense.[5]

— cosmologist Stephen Hawking

If it could be shown to you through solid and persuasive
evidence that God created the universe and everything in it,
and continues to play a significant role in that creation, would
you believe it?

Footnotes

1 Stephen Hawking, *A Brief History of Time* (New York, NY: Bantam,
   1998), introduction by Carl Sagan.
2 This paragraph is derived largely from Erwin W. Lutzer, *Seven Reasons Why You Can Trust the Bible* (Chicago, IL: Moody Press, 1998).
3 Lee Strobel, *The Case for Christ* (Grand Rapids, MI: Zondervan, 1998).
4 American Athiests Website, <http://www.atheists.org/bone.pit/
   creationscience.html>.
5 John Boslough, *Stephen Hawking's Universe* (New York, NY: Quill,
   1985).

—◦◦—

CHAPTER ONE

THE WORLD'S RELIGIONS

HOW DID THE WORLD'S MAJOR RELIGIONS COME INTO BEING?

While philosophy and religion are often looked to for moral guidance, major claims concerning the cause, nature, and purpose of the universe cannot go unnoticed. When science falls short, people turn to the suppositions of philosophy or to the supernatural of religion. What is life's ultimate purpose? Is God the Creator Almighty?

Undoubtedly, many modern people would boldly demand that such questions lie outside the realm of science, and are therefore unanswerable. Of course, others might claim that Hinduism or Buddhism or Islam or Judaism or Christianity contains all the correct answers.

But what really determines the credibility of any one religion or belief system is the underlying foundation upon which it is built. Just as a house's stability can only be as dependable as the foundation upon which it is constructed, so a belief system may only be as reliable as the foundation upon which it is based.

In addition to summarizing some central doctrines, this first chapter briefly explains how several of the larger worldwide religions, or belief systems, came into being.[1]

HINDUISM

"The history of Hinduism began in India about 1500 B.C. Although its literature can be traced only to before 1000 B.C., evidence of Hinduism's earlier [background] is derived from archaeology, comparative philology, and comparative religion."[2] According to the *Encyclopedia Britannica*, Hinduism "is both a civilization and a congregation of religions; it has neither a beginning or founder, nor a central authority, hierarchy, or organization. Every attempt at a specific definition of Hinduism has proved unsatisfactory in one way or another, the more so because the finest scholars of Hinduism, including Hindus themselves, have emphasized different aspects of the whole."[3]

As a religion, Hinduism involves a combination of diverse doctrines and ways of life; orthodox Hinduism includes an extraordinarily wide selection of beliefs and practices. Hinduism can include:

pantheism —   belief which identifies the universe
                 with God

polytheism —   the belief in many gods

monotheism —   the belief that there is only one God

14

agnosticism — the belief that the ultimate cause and the essential nature of things are unknown or unknowable or that human knowledge is limited to experience

atheism — the denial or disbelief in the existence of any God or gods

dualism — the belief that there are two independent divine beings or eternal principles, one good and the other evil

pluralism — recognizing more than one ultimate substance or principle

monism — the belief in one ultimate substance or principle, such as mind or matter, or the ground of both

Hindus' "only universal obligation, if they are orthodox, is to abide by the rules of their caste [hereditary social divisions] and trust that by doing so, their next birth will be a happier one."[4]

BUDDHISM

Born about 560 B.C. as a prince, son of a king in India, Buddha was married at the age of 19 and had a son in his late twenties. With a growing interest in matters of religion, he left the life of a householder at that time, and went on to search for true salvation. For six years he searched along the two most widely recognized roads to salvation known to India: philosophic meditation and bodily asceticism (life without pleasures), but he yielded no results.

So Buddha decided to take a new approach. He entered into a process of meditation at the foot of a tree (a tree which came to be known most simply as the Bo-tree) and said to himself determinedly, "Though skin, nerves, and bone shall waste away, and life-blood itself be dried up, here sit I till I attain enlightenment."[5]

And then suddenly the answer came to him: The stumbling block to his own salvation, and the cause of all human misery, was *desire*, too intense desire (*tanha,* "thirst," "craving,") — desire for the wrong things, arising out of the carnal will-to-live-and-have. As this insight grew within him, Buddha realized that *he was now without desire.* He realized that he was the Enlightened One. As he said "I have lived the highest life."[6]

Following his experience of enlightenment, Buddha had a discussion lasting several days with five of his former colleagues, during which he opened to them this experience. He challenged the five to believe his testimony, to admit that he was an "arahat" (a monk who had experienced enlightenment), and to try to become arahats themselves. The five people were converted, and thus the Buddhist monastic order came into being.

While Buddha wandered about preaching, other conversions continued to follow, until the number rose to 60, and eventually multiplied into the thousands. And as the numbers grew, so did the Buddhist Order rulebook, in which Buddha continually added rules and regulations to organize his newfound religion.[7]

Religiously, Buddha's interests were not so much in speculative philosophy, but rather in the realm of psychology, as the Buddhist records transmit: "Bear always in mind what it is that I have not made clear, and what it is that I have made clear. And what have I not made clear? I have not made clear that the world is eternal; I have not made clear that the world is not eternal; I have not made clear that the world is finite; I have not made clear that the world is infinite; I have not made clear that the soul and the body are identical; I have not made clear that the monk who has attained (the arahat) exists after death; I have not made clear that the arahat does not exist after death; I have not made clear that the arahat both exists and does not exist after death; I have not made clear that the arahat neither exists nor does not exist after death. And why have I not made this clear? Because this profits not, nor has to do with the fundamentals of religion; therefore I have not made this clear."[8]

Buddha did, however, believe that the universe abounded in gods, goddesses, demons, and other nonhuman powers, whom he believed to be subject to death and rebirth, just as humans were. He also believed in the "law of karma" and in the transmigration of souls. (He later modified both these doctrines, however.)

After 45 years of preaching, teaching, and constructive planning, Buddha's life ended unexpectedly after a meal of pork brought on a sudden mortal illness.[9]

ISLAM

Arabia encompassed a variety of religions before the advent of Islam. In Southern Arabia, an astral cult known as Sabaeanism prevailed. In other regions, there were Jews and Christians. But the great majority of Arabs worshiped local gods and goddesses, and believed in angels, fairies, and demonic jinn.

The year A.D. 570 marked the beginning of a whole new set of beliefs for the Arab people, when Muhammad, the founder of Islam, was born.

Growing up, Muhammad became disturbed by continuous quarreling over matters of religion and honor among the religious chiefs. Muhammad felt a great need to resolve his religious doubts, and would spend days at a time alone in a cave near the base of Mount Hira.

Suddenly one night (Muslims call it "The Night of Power and Excellence"), there rose in a vision before him an angel who claimed to be Gabriel, the messenger of God. Muhammad rushed home afterward in great excitement, half-doubting and half-believing. At first Muhammad had fears for his own sanity,[10] but after a period of self-questioning and discouragement lasting for several months, he came to look upon himself as a true prophet and messenger of Allah (Allah is the Arabic word for God).

Thus marked the beginning of the Koran, Muhammad's complete revelation in writing. Muslims (those who adhere to the Islamic faith) recognize both the Koran and much of the Christian Bible as inspired revelations from God. Both books agree that God has spoken through a long series of prophets, from Abraham to Jesus, and all those in between. But the Koran adds Muhammad to the end of the list, making him God's final and most important prophet in the series.[11]

In likeness to the Christian Bible, the Koran describes Jesus as a virgin-born, miracle-working Messiah, and also identifies Him as "holy" or "faultless." Unlike the Christian Bible, however, the Koran forbids worshiping Jesus as God. Muhammad taught that Jesus was no more than God's messenger, and that God does not have a Son.[12] As well, Jesus did not die on a cross, most Muslims believe, but rather, prior to His scheduled crucifixion, God raised Him to heaven so that He could not be seized. Approved Muslim commentaries suggest that perhaps Judas, the betrayer of Jesus, was actually the one who was crucified. Judas would have been supernaturally disguised so well that even Mary (Jesus' mother) and Jesus' followers were deceived.[13]

These new teachings at the time successfully converted only about 40 people in the first four years of the religion, but by A.D. 630, Muhammad had the company of close to ten thousand people by his side. Following his sudden death two years later, the religion of Islam spread rapidly, due largely to victory in battle and military conquest, in what is called the *jihad* ("holy war" or "holy struggle").[14]

As the second largest religion in the world today, devout Muslims strictly adhere to the Koran's prescribed five religious acts of obedience that will help ensure one's entry into heaven.[15] Known as Islam's "Five Pillars," these acts are:

1) Repetition of the Creed: "There is no god but Allah; and Muhammad is the prophet of Allah."

2) Prayer.

3) Almsgiving. In the early days of Islam this was a yearly tax, used as charity for the poor and repairs and administrative expenses for mosques [Muslim places of worship].

4) The fast during the sacred month of Ramadan, during which Muslims must abstain from food.

5) The pilgrimage to Mecca once in a lifetime.

JUDAISM

The primary source of information regarding the origin of Judaism is found in the *Tanakh* (the Old Testament portion of the Christian Bible[16]). The story of the first Jewish person, *Abraham*, who is considered the father of the Jews, is told in the Old Testament biblical Book of Genesis.[17] According to the account, God declared Abraham righteous because of his faith (Gen. 15:6). God chose Abraham and made a covenant with him: Abraham would be the father of not just one nation, but a multitude of nations with descendants as numerous as the stars. This covenant was to be everlasting from generation to generation. God also promised Abraham that his descendants would have their own land (some of which is modern Israel). As a sign that they had accepted the covenant, Abraham and his descendants were to circumcise each male among them. This covenant was confirmed through Abraham's second son, Isaac, and through his descendants, who are today's Jews.

Today, a Jew is any person whose mother was a Jew. It is important to note, however, that being Jewish does not necessarily have anything to do with what one believes or what one does. A person born to non-Jewish parents who believes everything that Orthodox Jews believe and observes every law and custom of Judaism is still a non-Jew, even in the eyes of the most liberal movements of Judaism.[18] A person born to a Jewish mother who is an atheist and never practices the Jewish religion is still a Jew, even in the eyes of the ultra-Orthodox. In this sense, being Jewish is more like a nationality than a religion.

Jews regard actions as more important than beliefs, although there is certainly a place for belief within Judaism. The closest that anyone has ever come to creating a widely accepted list of Jewish beliefs is Maimonides' 13 principles of faith. Maimonides' 13 principles of faith, which he thought were the minimum requirements of Jewish belief, are as follows:

1. God exists.

2. God is one and unique.

3. God is incorporeal [having no material body or form].

4. God is eternal.

5. Prayer is to be directed to God alone and to no other.

6. The words of the prophets are true.

7. Moses' prophecy supercedes that of any other prophet.

8. The written Torah and oral Torah were given to Moses [teachings that are contained in the Tanakh and other Jewish writings].

9. There will be no other Torah.

10. God knows the thoughts and deeds of men.

11. God will reward the good and punish the wicked.

12. The Messiah [Savior] will come.

13. The dead will be resurrected.

These are very basic and general principles. Yet as basic as these principles are, the necessity of believing in each one of them has been disputed at one time or another by various Jewish movements; the liberal movements of Judaism dispute many of them. All movements of Judaism, however, forbid belief in the Christian Bible's New Testament;[19] only the Bible's Old Testament portion (known as the Tanakh) is accepted, along with the Talmud (a collection of Jewish law and commentary).

Although beliefs are important within Judaism, actions are regarded as more important. According to Orthodox Judaism, these actions include 613 commandments given by God in the Tanakh, as well as laws instituted by the rabbis (the Jewish religious teachers), and long-standing customs such as the well-known Bar Mitzvah that almost every 13-year-old Jewish boy experiences.

The most famous of these 613 commandments are the Ten Commandments, which the Bible states God himself supernaturally engraved on tablets of stone. Many of these commandments, such as "Do not murder" and "Do not steal," serve to form the basis of morality in almost all cultures today.

The biblical Book of Exodus contains one of the most famous stories of the Bible, a story which has recently been dramatized by Hollywood in the feature film *The Prince of Egypt*. Around the second millennium B.C., when the Hebrews had become slaves in the land of Egypt, God came to the rescue. Through a man named Moses, God performed many wondrous miracles which compelled the stubborn Egyptian ruler to finally let the Hebrews go free. Here is a brief description of these miracles, in chronological order:

1) Water turning into blood

2) Vast hordes of frogs sweeping across Egypt, so many that even ovens and beds were filled with them

3) Dust turning into swarms of gnats

4) Swarms of flies sweeping through Egypt (as with the frogs), but not in Goshen (where the Hebrews lived)

5) A deadly plague afflicting only Egypt's livestock (horses, donkeys, camels, cattle, and sheep), but not the Hebrews's livestock

6) Animals and people of Egypt breaking out with terrible boils

7) A severe hailstorm covering only Egypt (but not where the Jews lived), worse than any in Egypt's history, destroying everything in the fields — people, animals, trees, and crops alike

8) Locusts covering the entire country — so many that people couldn't see the ground — and devouring everything that escaped the hailstorm.

9) A terrible darkness descending on the land of Egypt for three days, with the exception of the Hebrew areas

10) A deathly plague killing all the first-born sons of every family in Egypt, with the exception of Hebrew families, who were unaffected by this plague (this event is known today as the Jewish holiday called *Passover*, when death "passed over" the Hebrews and only killed the Egyptians)

11) And finally, the escape of the Hebrews through the Red Sea, where a path opened up before the people through the water, and all the people walked through on dry ground.

The Exodus account states that God caused these miracles to happen so that the people might see His power, and so that

His fame might spread throughout the earth (Exod. 9:16), causing people to believe in Him.

CHRISTIANITY

The Christian Bible, a collection of 66 books, from Genesis to Revelation, known as the Old and New Testaments, was written by over 40 authors covering a span of about 1,500 years. The New Testament portion of the Bible is the primary source of history regarding the origin of Christianity, and forms the basis of all Christian doctrine.

The first four books of the New Testament, known as the Gospels, are concerned primarily with telling the story of Jesus Christ. According to the Gospels, Jesus, the central figure and founder of Christianity, claimed to be the only Son of God, who came down from heaven to earth in bodily form.

Jesus' mission was to save mankind from their sins by dying a sacrificial death on the cross (known historically as the Crucifixion). The Bible teaches that Jesus' death was necessary because an innocent life had to substitute for the guilty. Holiness required that sin must not be ignored. As such, God sent His Son, Jesus, into the world to live an innocent life and pay the penalty for the sins of the world. Anyone who believes this, Jesus promised, would have eternal life with Him in heaven (John 3).

According to the New Testament, many people in the first century believed Jesus' claims to be the Son of God based on His supernatural power to perform miracles,[20] and also based on His resurrection from the dead. Jesus predicted His own death, but said that He would rise again three days later (Matt. 12:38–40), using this as His final proof that He spoke the truth.

Taken from the New Testament, the main doctrines of Christianity today are as follows:[21]

- Jesus Christ, God the Son, was born of the virgin Mary and received a human body and a sinless human nature, and in Him perfect humanity and divine nature are found in one personality.

- There is only one true and living God, an infinite, intelligent Spirit, the creator, ruler, and sustainer of the universe.

- The godhead eternally exists in three persons — the Father, the Son, and the Holy Spirit. These three are one God, having precisely the same nature, attributes, and perfections, and are worthy of the same honor, confidence, and obedience. Together, the three persons of the godhead execute distinct but harmonious offices in the work of the creation as well as redemption.

- Jesus Christ was crucified, buried, and then resurrected to life for the sins of all mankind, and He will return personally and bodily to make the Final Judgement of both believers and non-believers.

- People were originally created in the image and likeness of God. They fell short of the glory of God because of sin, and only through repentance of their sins and acceptance of Jesus Christ as their Savior and Lord will they inherit eternal life, or else suffer eternal condemnation.

- Jesus performed many miracles while living on earth to exhibit His divine nature. These included the resurrection of people from the dead, healing the blind, etc.

- The Bible was written without error by certain people throughout history, under the special inspiration of God, who is the ultimate author of the text. The Bible is the only complete revelation of the truth of God and the final authority for all Christian faith and practice.

As a result of such sensational beliefs, the claims of the New Testament have by and large become one of the most controversial scholarly debates of modern times. The New Testament has been more thoroughly studied by inquiring minds than any other book written. There are more translations of the Bible into different languages than any other book. There are more ancient, handwritten copies of the Bible still in existence than any other ancient writing.

The impact of Christianity in the first century was such that it became the officially accepted faith of the Western world for the next 1,700 years. The Canadian Constitution declares the supremacy of God in its first sentence: "Whereas Canada is founded upon the principles that recognize the supremacy of God and the rule of law. . . ." Likewise, the United States Declaration of Independence recognizes God (the Creator) in its second paragraph: "We hold these Truths to be self-evident, that all Men are created equal, that they are endowed by their Creator. . . ." And, of course, all U.S. currency is imprinted with the slogan "In God We Trust." The Christian Bible is often used in law courts for the taking of an oath of truth (in Canada and the United States). Amazingly, the Bible remains the number one selling book of all time.

Year after year, North America's popular culture recognizes and celebrates many Christian holidays: the most well-known, of course, is Christmas, celebrated as Jesus Christ's birthday (hence the word *Christ*mas). Next is Palm Sunday, celebrated as the day Jesus made His grand entrance into Jerusalem, then Good Friday, in remembrance of Jesus' death on the Cross, and finally Easter Sunday, in remembrance of His resurrection three days later.[22]

Finally, the year A.D. 2000 marks two thousand years since Jesus' ministry on earth (A.D. stands for *Anno Domini*, which is Latin for "in the year of our Lord"). Indeed, why *did* the life of Jesus change history from B.C. to A.D. two millennia ago?

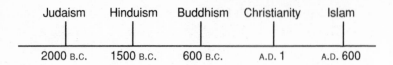

Judaism	Hinduism	Buddhism	Christianity	Islam
2000 B.C.	1500 B.C.	600 B.C.	A.D. 1	A.D. 600

Above: General timeline showing the rise
of each of today's major world religions

Footnotes

1 The information in this chapter is derived primarily from *Man's Religions*, by John B. Noss, professor of philosophy at Franklin and Marshall College (New York, NY: Macmillan Company, Revised Edition, 1961).

2 "The History of Hinduism," Encyclopedia Britannica Online, <http://members.eb.combol/topic?eu=108344&sctn=9>

3 "Hinduism," Encyclopedia Britannica Online, <http://members.eb.com/bol/topic?eu=108344&sctn=1>

4 Noss, *Man's Religions*, p. 114.

5 Ibid., p. 161.

6 Ibid., p. 162.

7 Ibid., p. 163–165.

8 Ibid., p. 166.

9 Today there are several forms of modernized Buddhism practiced primarily throughout the Asian world.

10 Noss, *Man's Religions*, p. 692–693.

11 It would be expected then, that Muhammad's message be consistent with that of the previous prophets.

12 According to the Christian Bible's New Testament, Jesus contrarily taught that He *was* the Son of God.

13 The Christian Bible teaches that it was Jesus who was crucified, a foundational doctrine for all Christian belief. The Bible says that Judas hung himself in guilt for betraying Jesus to the Cross.

14 Noss, *Man's Religions*, p. 710; see also "Islam," Encyclopedia Britannica Online, <http://members.eb.com/bol/topic?eu=108138&sctn=2>
There is division even amongst Muslims about how exactly to define jihad. For instance, many believe that it is appropriate to engage in war in defense of Islam, while a growing number believe jihad refers only to a "spiritual" battle and has no place in the material world.

15 It should be noted that in contradiction to Muhammad's teaching of salvation through specific acts of obedience, Jesus taught a message

of salvation through faith alone. Muslims often explain the differences between the Koran and the Christian Bible by suggesting that, over time, the text of the Bible has been tampered with. The argument for such tampering generally occurs where the teachings and predictions of Jesus do not line up with the teachings of Muhammad.

16 The Christian Bible is made up of two major parts: the Old Testament and the New Testament. The Old Testament, called the *Tanakh* by the Jewish people, was written in the period before the rise of Christianity. While the Christian faith is based on both the Old and New Testaments, the Judaic faith is based on only the Old Testament portion; Judaism rejects the teachings of the New Testament.

17 The authenticity of the area and era in which this biblical narrative takes place has been confirmed by recent archaeological discoveries, and dates to approximately 2000 B.C. ("Abraham," Encyclopedia Britannica Online, <http://members.eb.com/bol/topic?eu=3413&sctn=1>)

18 However, if a person has gone through the formal process of conversion to Judaism, he or she may be considered Jewish.

19 The writers of the Bible's Old Testament prophesied of a future Savior (Messiah) who would come to rule the world with righteousness and justice. Judaism rejects Jesus as the fulfillment of this prophecy, whereas Christianity accepts Jesus as the prophesied Messiah who died and rose again, and who will return in the last days to rule the world.

20 Such miracles included healing the blind, healing the crippled, walking on water, and more.

21 Groups such as the Jehovah's Witnesses and the Mormons that reject some of these central teachings of the New Testament *cannot* be, and are not considered, Christian denominations.

22 As at Christmas, so also at Easter, popular customs reflect many ancient pagan survivals — in this instance, connected with spring fertility rites, such as the symbols of the Easter egg and the Easter bunny. ("Easter," Encyclopedia Britannica Online, <http:/members.eb.com/bol/topic?eu=108313&sctn=14>)

CHAPTER
TWO

THE ANTHROPIC PRINCIPLE

DO SCIENTISTS THINK THAT THE UNIVERSE APPEARS TO HAVE BEEN DESIGNED?

The subject of the creation of the universe has been debated and pondered by people for centuries. Today, scientists continue to move forward in their quest to discover the true origin of mankind. One discovery that has intrigued many for the last few decades is something called the "anthropic principle."

The anthropic principle may be taken to mean that scientists have discovered a very large number of coincidences in the universe that allow life to exist on this planet. In other words, the universe *appears* to have been created specifically for the existence of life on earth. For a better idea of what this entails, consider the following examples:[1]

- If the earth was located only slightly farther away from the sun, it would freeze like the planet Mars. If it was only slightly closer, it would burn up in heat like the 860°F temperature on Venus.

- If the earth did not revolve regularly on its axis, half of the planet would be in permanent darkness without vegetation. Meanwhile, the other side of the planet would be an uninhabitable desert, suffering from the overwhelming heat of permanent exposure to the sun.

- If the Earth were not tilted at 23°, it would not have the seasonal variation that produces the abundance of crops that feed the planet's huge population. Without this tilt, less than half of the present land used for cultivation of crops would grow vegetables.

- If the earth was only a small percentage smaller, the reduced gravity would be incapable of holding the atmosphere that is essential for breathing.

- If the planet Earth was twice as large, the effect of increased gravity would make everything on the planet's surface weigh eight times what it weighs today. This increased weight would destroy many forms of animal and human life.

- A much thinner atmosphere would provide no protection from the 25,000 meteors that burn up over the earth every day. A thinner atmosphere would also be incapable of retaining the higher temperatures required for the existence of human and animal life.

- If the atmosphere were not 78 percent nitrogen and 22 percent oxygen and other gases, breathing would be impossible.

- If nuclear forces were decreased by only a few percent, the particles of the universe could not have come together in nuclear reactions to make the ingredients from which life must be constructed (such as carbon atoms).

- If the combined masses of the proton and electron were a little more rather than a little less than the mass of the neutron, the effect would be devastating. The hydrogen atom would become unstable. Throughout the universe, all the hydrogen atoms would immediately break down to form neutrons and neutrinos. Robbed of its nuclear fuel, the sun would fade and collapse. Across the whole of space, stars like the sun would contract in their billions, releasing a deadly flood of x-rays as they burned out. By that time, life on earth, needless to say, would already have been extinguished.

The ultimate conclusion is that if the universe was changed in the slightest way, no life could exist. (Although the possibility remains that other forms of *unknown* life might be able to exist, even the evolutionary cosmologist Stephen Hawking stresses, "It seems clear that there are relatively few ranges of values [for these coincidences] that would allow the development of *any* form of intelligent life."[2]) Thus, more than a few scientists think that this chain of "coincidences" could at the very least suggest the work of a Creator or "creative force." Hawking, one of the world's most respected cosmologists, remarks, "I think there are clearly religious implications whenever you start to discuss the origins of the universe. There must be religious overtones. But I think most scientists prefer to shy away from the religious side of it."[3]

The book *Stephen Hawking's Universe* concludes that the odds against the accidental formation of a universe such as this would be comparable to shaking the parts of a watch in a barrel and having them fall into place as a working timepiece.[4] What implications could these incredible probabilities entail? Well, if one can determine how unlikely it is that a given pattern can arise by chance, one has his or her answer as to how likely it is that the structure is deliberate. Here is a simplified example for illustration:

Suppose you find a quarter lying on the street. Without a moment's thought, you assume that someone dropped it accidentally — that it's there "by chance." You assume this because it's so commonplace an occurrence. After all, consider the alternative: that someone placed it there deliberately. Though it's theoretically possible, your own personal experience tells you that it's pretty unlikely.

Now, what if you found three quarters, all close to one another? Still, it seems more likely that someone dropped a cluster of coins by accident, than that the person put them there. (Maybe you feel it's a close call.) Part of this calculation (which is less certain than the prior one) involves something else, too: a reasonable guess about people's reasons for doing things. It's hard to think of a good reason for someone putting three quarters on the ground deliberately.

Let's take it one step further. Suppose you again find three quarters, but this time they are all touching one another, forming a triangular arrangement. Was this deliberate, or by chance? Chance certainly can't be ruled out, but it seems "suspicious." It's now likely that you'll change your mind and think that someone did it "on purpose" — even though the purpose is hard to imagine.

Finally, what if you find ten quarters stacked neatly one on top of another? Though once again you can't prove it didn't "just happen," the odds against it will seem so great (*It's so odd,* you'll think) that you'll be certain the stack was placed there for some unknown reason.[5]

And so it is with the properties of the universe. Rather than an enormous accident, the hundreds of "coincidences" observed throughout the universe may constitute a deliberate pattern. Many scientists think that the best explanation is "intelligent design." The renowned science writers John Gribbin and Martin Rees note, "This combination of coincidences . . . is indeed remarkable. There is no better evidence to support the argument that the universe has been designed for our benefit — tailor-made for man."[6]

Nobel Prize winner Max Planck, whose research revolutionized today's understanding of atomic and subatomic processes, just as Albert Einstein's theory of relativity revolutionized today's understanding of space and time,[7] concluded, "According to everything taught by the exact sciences about the immense realm of nature, a certain order prevails — one independent of the human mind. . . . This order can be formulated in terms of purposeful activity. There is evidence of an intelligent order of the universe to which both man and nature are subservient."[8]

Footnotes

1 There are literally hundreds of examples. Many of the examples as listed here are derived from *The Signature of God* by Grant Jeffrey (Nashville, TN: Word, 1996). These facts or "coincidences" are supported by highly recognized and noted cosmologists and physicists such as Sir Martin Rees, John Gribbin, Stephen Hawking, Alan Lightman, George Greenstein, John Barrow, Frank Tipler, Sir Frederick Hoyle, and others.

2 Stephen Hawking, *The Illustrated A Brief History of Time* (New York, NY: Bantam Books, 1996), p. 160; emphasis added.

3 John Boslough, *Stephen Hawking's Universe* (New York, NY: Quill, 1985). To avoid confusion, Hawking is not here advocating any particular belief; he is simply stressing in general terms the metaphysical implications of the origins of the universe.

4 Boslough, *Stephen Hawking's Universe*.

5 Illustration taken from Jeffrey Satinover, *Cracking the Bible Code* (New York, NY: W. Morrow, 1997).

6 John Gribbin and Martin Rees, *Cosmic Coincidences* (New York, NY: Bantam Books, 1989), p. 247. Some (including Gribbin and Rees themselves) argue that this explanation is just one of many other possible explanations which may evade us. The most popular alternative explanation to "intelligent design" is the "many worlds" view. In this view, our universe is but one in a vast ensemble of universes, and just by chance ours happens to be life-permitting. However, there is no evidence for such additional universes; in fact, no evidence is even possible. Some objections to the "many worlds" view are raised in Stephen Hawking's *A Brief History of Time*. See Stephen Hawking, *The Illustrated A Brief History of Time* (New York, NY: Bantam Books, 1996), p. 161.

7 Max Planck, Encyclopedia Britannica Online, <http://members.eb.com/bol/topic?eu=115045&sctn=1>

8 Aron Barth, *The Creation in the Light of Modern Science* (Jerusalem: Religious Section of the Youth and Hechalutz Dept. of the Zionist Organization, 1968).

———•◦•———

CHAPTER THREE

TWO WORLD VIEWS IN CONFLICT

WHAT DO THOUSANDS OF SCIENTISTS BELIEVE ABOUT CREATION AND EVOLUTION?

When discussing the topic of the *origins* of life, most people associate *evolution* with science, and *creation* with religion. *Evolution* is the scientific explanation, while *creation* is the religious one. These two viewpoints, evolution and creation, have today become the major competing explanations regarding life's origins.

The theory of creation (sometimes called scientific creationism) says that the universe and living organisms originated from specific acts of divine creation as told in the biblical account. This theory was prevalent in the mid 19th century until Charles Darwin first introduced the theory of evolution in his 1859 publication, *Origin of Species*. This new theory of evolution hypothesized that, from non-living matter, simple living organisms formed and progressed naturally into complex ones.

Today the theory of evolution has become widely known as the only scientific explanation for the origin of life, and the theory of creation is commonly understood to be based solely on religious beliefs. This is because there seems to be a lack of scientific evidence supporting the biblical claims of creation, while evolution appears to be supported by a vast body of scientific evidence. As a result, most educational institutes teach the theory of evolution as the sole explanation for human origins.

However, in recent years there has been a growing number of scientists who reject evolution, as new research has begun to seriously call into question some of the dogmatic beliefs of evolutionary theory. There are now thousands of fully accredited scientists around the world, and the number continues to rise, who believe there is more evidence to support creation than evolution. In fact, while many new discoveries are being made, the evidence used largely against creation, and in support of evolution, appears to be quickly crumbling. The weight of the evidence is shifting so steeply that as recently as 1999, one school board in the United States banned the testing of the theory of evolution from its science curriculum.[1]

The media has generally laughed at this decision, alleging it was made on a purely religious basis, yet the evidence used is strong. Some of the main arguments against evolution and for creation are presented on the following pages of this chapter.[2]

The Experts Say What?

In 1981, the British Museum of Natural History in London, England, to mark its one hundredth anniversary, opened a new exhibit on evolution. As one entered the exhibition hall, one saw a notice in flickering lights:

Have you ever wondered why there are so many different kinds of living things?

One idea is that all the living things we see today have EVOLVED from a distant ancestor by a process of gradual change.

How could evolution have occurred? How could one species change into another?

The exhibition in this hall looks at one possible explanation — the explanation first thought of by Charles Darwin.

One of the world's leading scientific journals, *Nature*, promptly ran an editorial in response to the museum's suggestion above that evolution by natural selection was only one of a number of possible explanations. The editorial was titled "Darwin's Death in South Kensington."[3] The editor quoted a phrase from a brochure of the museum, "If the theory of evolution is true," as evidence of the Museum's "rot." It continued:

The new exhibition policy, the museum's chief interaction with the outside world, is being developed in some degree of isolation from the museum's staff of distinguished biologists, most of whom would rather lose their right hands than begin a sentence with the phrase, "If the theory of evolution is true. . . ."

Two weeks later, this editorial solicited the following response from the museum:

> Sir — As working biologists at the British Museum of Natural History we were astonished to read your editorial "Darwin's Death in South Kensing-ton." How is it that a journal such as yours that is devoted to science and its practice can advocate that theory be presented as fact? This is the stuff of prejudice, not science, and as scientists our basic concern is to keep an open mind on the unknowable. Surely it should not be otherwise?
>
> You suggest that most of us would rather lose our right hands than begin a sentence with the phrase "If the theory of evolution is true. . . ." Are we to take it that evolution is a fact, proven to the limits of scientific rigor? If that is the inference then we must disagree most strongly. We have no absolute proof of the theory of evolution. What we do have is overwhelming circumstantial evidence in favor of it and as yet no better alternative. But the theory of evolution would be abandoned tomorrow if a better theory appeared.[4]

The letter was signed by 22 of the museum's staff of "distinguished biologists."

Other experts have also made some significant comments concerning the theory of evolution.

The great evolutionist Theodosius Dobzhansky, whose work had a major influence on 20th century thought and research on genetics and evolutionary theory,[5] published a review of a book entitled *Evolution du Vivant (Evolution of Living Organisms)*. This book was written by one of the most distinguished of French scientists, Pierre P. Grassé.

In Dobzhansky's review of Grassé's book, he stated, "The book of Pierre P. Grassé is a frontal attack on all kinds of Darwinism. Its purpose is to destroy the myth of evolution as a simple, understood, and explained phenomenon, and to show that evolution is a mystery about which little is, and perhaps can be, known. Now, one can disagree with Grassé but not ignore him. He is the most distinguished of French zoologists, the editor of the 28 volumes of 'Traite de Zoologie,' author of numerous original investigations, and ex-president of the Academie des Sciences. His knowledge of the living world is encyclopedic. . . ." And in the closing sentence of the review, Dobzhansky says, "The sentence with which Grassé ends his book is disturbing: 'It is possible that in this domain biology, impotent, yields the floor to metaphysics.' " In other words, Grassé closes his book with the statement that biology is powerless to explain the origin of living things, and that it may have to yield to metaphysics, possibly supernatural creation of some kind.[6]

Grassé, with an encyclopedic knowledge in the field, argued that "the explanatory doctrines of biological evolution do not stand up to an objective in-depth criticism. They prove to be either in conflict with reality, or else incapable of solving the major problem involved."[7]

A startling statement by Professor Louis Bounoure declared, "Evolution is a fairy tale for grown-ups. This theory has helped nothing in the progress of science. It is useless."[8] Bounoure was former president of the Biological Society of Strasbourg and director of the Strasbourg Zoological Museum, and later Director of Research at the French National Center of Scientific Research.

LIFE FROM NON-LIFE

The basis for evolution led to a revival of the spontaneous biogenesis theory, also known as chemical evolution, or spontaneous generation. Spontaneous generation is the hypothetical process by which living organisms develop from nonliving matter. However, this concept was disproved by Louis Pasteur, whose contributions were among the most valuable in the history of science.[9] Pasteur proved through famous experiments that all life comes from life, never from non-life.[10]

There has never been a scientific experiment that has produced pure samples of the correct type of proteins or nucleotides necessary for the production of life. However, in 1953 the famous Miller/Urey experiment proved that in a hypothetical primordial atmosphere, ammonia, water, methane, and energy can combine to form some amino acids which are required for life. Yet the highly praised Miller/Urey experiment did not produce any of the fundamental building blocks of life itself. It produced 85 percent tar, 13 percent carbolic acid, 1.05 percent glycine, 0.85 percent alanine, and trace amounts of other chemicals. Although the amino acids glycine and alanine are required for life, the tar and carbolic acids would be toxic to any proteins if they ever formed. Every subsequent experiment of this kind has produced similar results. Some experiments have produced slightly higher percentages of the usable product, but the majority of the material that is produced by these experiments is toxic to life.[11]

In fact, the *Encyclopedia Britannica* has affirmed in one article that modern findings "pose grave difficulties" for spontaneous generation theories supported by the famous Miller/Urey experiment.[12] Moreover, many scientists now believe that the earth's early atmosphere would have made the synthesis of organic molecules virtually impossible in the Miller/Urey experiment. For example, NASA has reported that a "reducing atmosphere" has never existed, although the experiment assumes one.[13] It is also now realized that the ultraviolet radiation from sunlight is destructive to any developing life. And there are many other specific criticisms of the Miller/Urey experiment as well that show its fundamental assumptions about the primordial atmosphere to be false.[14]

Despite the accumulating evidence that stacks up against the Miller/Urey experiment, it is nonetheless still used in educational institutes worldwide to support the idea that life was spontaneously produced from non-life.

The evolutionist and Nobel Prize winner George Wald demonstrates this inconsistency very clearly: "Spontaneous generation of a living organism is impossible. Yet here we [human beings] are, as a result, I believe, of spontaneous generation."[15]

MUTATIONS — EVOLUTION'S RAW MATERIAL

Today it is often alleged that evolution is central to the science of biology. Without the theory of evolution, it is said, the science of biology would completely break down. But the simple fact that living creatures can physically change and adapt to their environments does not necessarily help to explain the *origin* of living things in the first place.

The theory of evolution says that a hypothetical first living cell (like a bacterium) evolved, over billions of years, into a human being. But such a process meant finding a way to generate enormous amounts of genetic information (DNA), including the instructions for making eyes, nerves, skin, bones, muscle, blood, etc. Thus, the total information content of the genetic code (DNA) must have continually increased with the emergence of new genes (or instructions).

What mechanism could possibly have added all the extra genetic instructions required to progressively transform a one-celled creature into a human being? Evolutionists believe it was something called genetic *mutations*.

The English language can be used as an analogy to illustrate what a genetic mutation is: The message "The enemy is now attacking" could mistakenly be copied as "The enemy is not attacking." Naturally, this mistake would probably result in harmful consequences. Indeed, it is unlikely that a random mistake might actually improve the meaning of the message; very likely the meaning would be damaged.[16]

In the same way, mutations are generally random copying mistakes in the reproduction of the genetic code (DNA), and as such, tend to be harmful. The code in DNA is simply a complex set of instructions that tells a creature's body how to reproduce itself (much the same as a set of instructions that tells a person how to reproduce a car or spaceship). Random copying mistakes (mutations), then, are obviously unlikely to improve these instructions; rather they are much more likely to damage or destroy them, as the *Encyclopedia Britannica* acknowledges.[17] That is why many mutations cause disease and death.[18] In fact, according to one university biology textbook, the odds that a mutation (random copying mistake) might actually improve the instructions contained in the genetic code are so low that "a random change is not likely to improve the genome (genetic code) any more than firing a gunshot blindly through the hood of a car is likely to improve engine performance."[19] But this isn't surprising, since mutations are random mistakes.

However, evolutionists generally believe that occasionally a "good" mutation will occur, one which *will* improve the genetic code, despite the overwhelming odds as described above. It is thought that such "good" copying mistakes would scramble the instructions in the code in such a way as to improve it, thus generating the new information required to tell the body how to build a new physical feature. Such "good" mutations, the *Encyclopedia Britannica* says, would "serve as the raw material of evolution."[20]

Evolutionists believe that over the last 4.5 billion years, an accumulation of trillions of these hypothetical "good" copying mistakes have continuously improved the genetic code, adding enough new information to transform a bacterium into a human being.

This is the equivalent of saying that random copying mistakes when re-typing the instructions to produce an automobile could eventually result in such an improved set of instructions, that instead of producing an automobile, the new and improved instructions would produce a working spaceship!

To summarize: evolutionists generally believe that new DNA information (genes) comes from "good" accidental copying mistakes, and these types of copying errors are what have generated the encyclopedic amounts of information necessary to transform the first self-reproducing organism billions of years ago into every living thing in the world today. In conjunction with a process called "natural selection," this makes up the "neo-Darwinian theory of evolution," today the most widely believed explanation among evolutionists for life's origins.[21]

Has a "good" mutation ever really been observed?

That is, has a mutation been observed which has been seen to improve the genetic code by adding meaningful information (new genes, or "instructions") to build (at least part of) a new physical feature?

It is first necessary to briefly define what is meant by the term "information" in this context. The DNA code has already been defined as a set of instructions, analogous to an English message. The sequence of "letters" (or bases) in the code is not random or repetitive, but instead, like the letters in a written message. In other words, the code has meaning. For instance, a random sequence of English letters such as "nkntweioeimytnhatcesga" means nothing, but when the same letters are arranged "the enemy is now attacking," it becomes a meaningful message, containing meaningful information.

It is the specific *arrangement* of letters that makes the message meaningful to someone who understands the language, and this meaningful arrangement is, in itself, "information." In the same way, it is the specific arrangement of "letters" (or bases) in the DNA code that makes the code meaningful to the body, which understands the DNA (genetic) language. This meaningful arrangement of "letters" in the DNA code is what makes up the information that tells the body how to produce a particular physical feature or characteristic, such as an eyeball or hair color.[22]

Today, there is a small handful of cases in which a genetic mutation has helped a creature to survive better than those without it. These types of mutations are referred to as "beneficial mutations." But even these beneficial mutations do not improve the code in DNA: rather than adding any meaningful information, they destroy it. For example, Darwin pointed to a case in which a genetic mutation caused flying beetles on a small desert island to lose their wings (the "wing-making" information in the DNA was lost or scrambled in some way). However, due to this loss, the beetles had a better chance of survival because they were less likely to be blown into the sea. Thus, the mutation was "beneficial" to the beetle population because it helped them to survive better in their environment. This shows how even a *beneficial mutation* can be damaging to the DNA code; in this case the mutation involved a loss or corruption of the information (or genes) for making wings.

Textbooks regularly use examples of beneficial mutations as evidence for evolution. But the problem with using beneficial mutations to support evolution is that they are exactly the opposite of what is required, that is, they involve a loss or corruption of existing information. For instance, losing the ability to fly has nothing to do with the origins of flight in the first place, which is what evolution is supposed to be about.

To produce a beetle from a simple cell, it is obvious that an increase of new genetic information is necessary to create the eyes, the wings, etc. Thus, to support evolution, the preceding beetle example would have to be reversed. The DNA code would have to be improved rather than damaged — new meaningful information (genes) would have to be produced. This means that a new physical feature would have to arise that was never before present — beetles normally born without wings would subsequently have to be born with them.[23] But no such example exists.

Some of the most common examples given as proof of beneficial mutations are those that cause pesticide and antibiotic resistance in rodents and bacteria. For instance, the book *Teaching about Evolution and the Nature of Science*, published by the National Academy of Sciences, states, "Many strains of bacteria have become increasingly resistant to antibiotics . . . [and] similar episodes of rapid evolution are occurring in many different organisms. Rats have developed resistance to the poison warfarin . . . [and] many hundreds of insect species and other agricultural pests have evolved resistance to the pesticides used to combat them."[24] Examples such as these are almost always used by textbooks to show "evolution happening." But like the wingless beetles, they are still the result of a loss of DNA information, or sometimes a transfer of existing information — not the result of new information.[25]

In fact, one recent discovery proved that in many cases bacteria *already* had the genes for resistance to certain antibiotics, even before those antibiotics were invented! Reuters News Service reported that one of the ways in which bacteria become resistant to antibiotics is by swapping genes among species. The mechanism by which they do this has been thought by many to have "evolved" in response to antibiotics. However, researchers have looked at preserved samples of cholera bacteria dating back to 1888. They found that the same gene-swapping mechanisms were already there — well before antibiotics were discovered or used by people![26]

Is there ever an addition of new information?

When one looks at all the textbook examples of evolution, there are none that cause an addition of new genetic (DNA) information. All appear to be downhill (information-losing) processes, contrary to what evolution requires. Refer to the illustration on the following page by creationist scientists of how genetic information is lost, rather than gained, as creatures adapt to their environment.

One of the most commonly used examples of evolutionary change is one which involves a population of "peppered moths" in England. Indeed, many museums[27] and educational institutes worldwide use this as one of the most striking examples of evolution ever witnessed by mankind. The story goes like this: Prior to the industrial revolution in England, the peppered moth population consisted predominantly of light-colored moths (containing speckled dots). A dark-colored form comprised only a small minority of the population. This was so because predators (birds) could more easily detect the dark-colored moths as they rested during the day on light-colored tree trunks. With the onset of the industrial revolution and resultant air pollution, the tree trunks and rocks became progressively darker. As a consequence, the dark-colored moths became increasingly difficult to detect, while the light-colored form ultimately became easy prey. Birds, therefore, began eating more light-colored than dark-colored moths, and today over 95 percent of the peppered moths in the industrial areas of England are of the darker-colored variety.

In this example, it is obvious that "natural selection" only changed the ratios of black and light (peppered) forms. Both varieties were already present in the population, so nothing new was produced (i.e., no new information or genes were

HOW INFORMATION IS LOST WHEN
CREATURES ADAPT TO THEIR ENVIRONMENT

In this simplified example for illustration, a single gene pair is shown under each bear as coming in to possible forms. One form of the gene (L) carried instructions for long fur, the other (S) for short fur. In row 1, we start with medium-furred animals (LS) interbreeding. Each of the offspring of these bears can get one of either gene from each parent to make up their two genes.

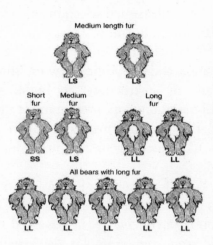

In row 2, we see that the resultant offspring can have either short (SS), medium (LS), or long (LL) fur. Now, imagine the climate cooling drastically (as in a post-Flood ice age). Only those with long fur survive to give rise to the next generation (line 3). So from then on, all the bears will be a new, long-furred variety. Note that:

1. They are now *adapted* to their environment.
2. They are now more *specialized* than their ancestors on row 1.
3. This has occurred through *natural selection*.
4. There have been *no new genes* added.
5. In fact, genes have been lost from the population — i.e., *there has been a loss of genetic information*, the opposite of what microbe-to-man evolution needs in order to be credible.
6. Now the population is less able to adapt to future environmental changes — were the climate to become hot, there is no genetic information for short fur, so the bears would probably overheat.

Illustration courtesy of Answers in Genesis, Florence, Kentucky.

added). Thus, like the wingless beetles, the example of the peppered moths does not actually support evolution, since evolution requires the emergence of new genes![28]

While natural selection and beneficial mutations "may increase an organism's adaptation,"[29] no one has ever been able to point to a mutation that has actually improved the genetic code by adding new meaningful information (new genes or "instructions" for building a new physical trait). All mutations appear to scramble the *already-existing* information (instructions), either by the reshuffling or duplication of existing genes, or simply by damaging the genes altogether.

Oxford professor Richard Dawkins is generally regarded as one of the most influential neo-Darwinists in the world. During an interview,[30] he was asked a crucial question: Could he point to any example today in which a mutation has actually added new genetic information? (If there is such an example, surely an Oxford zoology professor, promoting neo-Darwinism around the world, would know of it.) Dawkins appeared so perplexed by this question that the creation organization who produced the video says that "Dawkins' response on screen makes a more powerful point *against* evolution than volumes written by creationists."[31]

Another scientist, Dr. Ian Macreadie, winner of several scientific awards for outstanding contributions to molecular biological research, affirms that "all you see in the lab is either gene duplications, reshuffling of existing genes, or defective genes (with a loss of information). . . . But you never see any new information arising in a cell . . . we just don't observe it happening. It's hard to see how any serious scientist could believe that real information can arise just by itself, from nothing."[32]

But because examples such as the wingless beetles and the peppered moths show physical changes in living creatures, they are still repeatedly used by evolutionists to promote the idea that primitive bacteria have changed so much in the distant past that today they have become people. Yet such examples simply do not support evolution — all observed examples of change are either genetically neutral or genetically downhill, being losses of information instead of the required gains. Losing bits of genetic information a little at a time surely does not help explain how the genetic code was built in the first place; one can't build a business by losing a little bit of money at a time.

It's not surprising that one of the most well-known evolutionists openly criticized the traditional neo-Darwinian theory of evolution. On the faculties of Harvard and New York University, the late Stephen Jay Gould was the author of over 15 books on scientific topics and contributed monthly essays to the periodical *Natural History* since January 1974. His essays have also appeared in other scientific periodicals and his work can be found quoted in educational textbooks at all levels.[33] He wrote that although he had been "beguiled" by the unifying power of neo-Darwinism when he studied it as a graduate student in the 1960s, the weight of the evidence pushed him to the reluctant conclusion that neo-Darwinism "as a general proposition, is effectively dead, despite its persistence as textbook orthodoxy."[34]

Today, there is a growing realization that the presently accepted concept of natural selection and mutations really explains nothing of evolutionary significance. One leading creationist summarized the situation well: "All of our real-world experience, especially in today's 'information age,' would indicate that to rely on accidental copying mistakes to generate real information is the stuff of wishful thinking, not science."[35] In everyday experience, information never arises without an intelligent source.

FOSSILS

A fossil is a remnant, impression, or trace of an animal or plant that has been preserved in the earth. Usually, a fossil is simply the skeleton (or impression of the skeleton) of a dead creature preserved or molded in hardened rock.

It is agreed that the best and most likely way for a fossil to be produced is by the sudden burial of a creature in sediment or soil, at or soon after death.[36] If dead creatures remain on the surface of the ground or float in water, they will decay quickly or be eaten by other animals. Once buried in suitable soil, however, decay takes place very slowly leaving either the bones themselves or impressions of where the bones have been.

Paleontologists have recovered and studied the fossil remains of many thousands of organisms that lived in the past. The fossil record shows that many kinds of extinct organisms were very different in form from any now living.

According to evolutionary theory, the earliest fossils resemble micro-organisms such as bacteria and blue-green algae; the oldest ones appear in rocks 3,500,000,000 old. The oldest animal fossils, about 700,000,000 years old, come from small wormlike creatures with soft bodies. The first vertebrates, animals with backbones, appeared about 400,000,000 years ago, and the first mammals less than 200,000,000 years ago. The *Encyclopedia Britannica*, from an evolutionary viewpoint, states that "the history of life recorded by fossils presents compelling evidence of evolution."[37]

Now that 200 million fossil specimens have been catalogued of over 250,000 fossil species, the fossil record allows for meaningful analysis. If living things have in fact evolved from other kinds of creatures, then many intermediate or transitional forms of creatures, with halfway structures, should be evident in the fossil record. However, if God created different kinds of animals separately, as creationists believe, the fossil record should show creatures appearing abruptly and fully formed.

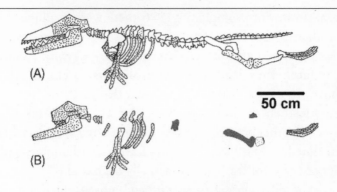

(A) Reconstruction of *Ambulocetus natans*, "at the end of the power stroke during swimming."
(B) The dotted bones were all that were actually found, and the shaded ones were found 5m above the rest. With the "additions" removed, there really isn't much left of *Ambulocetus!*

Illustration courtesy of Answers in Genesis, Florence, Kentucky.

Evolutionists point to a few transitional animal forms that they believe show evolutionary transition in the fossil record. However, such intermediates are often speculative and much disputed, even amongst evolutionists themselves. For example, one commonly used transitional form is the *Ambulocetus natans* ("walking whale that swims"), discovered recently. It is believed that whales evolved from some form of land mammal, and that the *Ambulocetus natans* is transitional between the two, with halfway structures between land mammal and whale. But when reconstructed fossil drawings of *Ambulocetus natans* are compared with the actual bones found, it is realized that the critical skeletal elements necessary to establish the transition from non-swimming land mammal to whale are missing![38] See diagram above.

The media often sensationalize fossil "proofs" of evolution reported in scientific journals. But when these journals later report disproofs of the same fossils, the media rarely mention it. For example, in 1996 there were headlines like "Feathered Fossil Proves Some Dinosaurs Evolved into Birds."[39] This was about a fossil called *Sinosauropteryx prima*. About a year later, four leading paleontologists, including Yale University's John Ostrom, found that the "feathers" were not really feathers at all — they were just a parallel array of fibers.[40] Another example is when the cover of *Time* magazine[41] illustrated a dino-bird link with feathers, although not the slightest trace of feathers had actually been found![42]

The *Encyclopedia Britannica* contains an interesting article on turtles which claims "the evolution of the turtle is one of the most remarkable in the history of the vertebrates." However, in the next sentence it states, "Unfortunately the origin of [the turtle] is obscured by the *lack of early fossils*, although *turtles leave more and better fossil remains than do other vertebrates*."[43] The article affirms that "intermediates between turtles and cotylosaurs, the primitive reptiles from which turtles probably sprang, are *entirely lacking*."[44]

If turtles leave "more and better fossil remains than do other vertebrates" but transitional forms are "entirely lacking," what can this say for intermediates between all other vertebrates?

In reality, the fossil record seems to fit the creation model well — the record is in fact characterized by abrupt appearances of fully formed organisms, with large systematic gaps (lacking transitional forms) between different types of creatures. Geologist David Raup, curator at Chicago's Field Museum of Natural History, explains, "Instead of finding the gradual unfolding of life, what geologists of Darwin's time, and geologists of the present day, actually find is a highly uneven or jerky record; that is, species appear in the sequence very suddenly, show little or no change during their existence in the record, then abruptly go out of the record."[45]

World-renowned evolutionary paleontologist Stephen Jay Gould further acknowledged, "New species almost always appeared suddenly in the fossil record with no intermediate links to ancestors in older rocks of the same region. . . . The extreme rarity of transitional forms in the fossil record persists as the trade secret of paleontology. The evolutionary trees that adorn our textbooks have data only at the tips and nodes of their branches; the rest is inference, however reasonable, not the evidence of fossils. . . . I regard the failure to find a clear 'vector of progress' in life's history as the most puzzling fact of the fossil record."[46]

Over a hundred years ago, Darwin pointed out the "fatal" significance of abrupt appearances and systematic gaps in the fossil record: "Why do we not find them [innumerable transitional forms] embedded in countless numbers in the crust of the earth? . . . If numerous species . . . have really started into life all at once, the fact would be fatal to the theory [of evolution]. . . . Why then is not every geological formation and every stratum full of such intermediate links? Geology assuredly does not reveal any such finely graduated organic chain; and this, perhaps, is the most obvious and gravest objection which can be urged against my theory. The explanation lies, as I believe, in the extreme imperfection of the geological record."[47]

But evolutionist Niles Eldredge[48] of the American Museum of Natural History said, "[Darwin] prophesied that future generations of paleontologists would fill in these gaps by diligent search. . . . One hundred and twenty years of paleontological research later, it has become abundantly clear that the fossil record will not confirm this part of Darwin's predictions. Nor is the problem a miserably poor record. The fossil record simply shows that this prediction was wrong."[49]

Geologist David Raup, supervisor of one of the largest fossil collections in the world, said that today "we have even fewer examples of evolutionary transition than we had in Darwin's time. . . . The evidence we find in the geologic record is not nearly as compatible with Darwinian natural selection as we would like it to be. Darwin was completely aware of this. He was embarrassed by the fossil record because it didn't look the way he predicted it would. . . . Some of the classic cases of Darwinian change in the fossil record, such as the evolution of the horse in North America, have had to be discarded or modified as the result of more detailed information."[50]

Niles Eldredge, again commenting on the acclaimed exhibit of horse evolution, states, "There have been an awful lot of stories, some more imaginative than others, about what the nature of that history [of life] really is. The most famous example, still on exhibit downstairs, is the exhibit on horse evolution prepared perhaps 50 years ago. That has been presented as the literal truth in textbook after textbook. Now I think that that is lamentable, particularly when the people who propose those kinds of stories may themselves be aware of the speculative nature of some of that stuff."[51]

A senior evolutionary paleontologist at the British Museum of Natural History, Colin Patterson[52] has also made some surprising statements about transitional fossils: "Gould and the American Museum people are hard to contradict when they say there are no transitional fossils. . . . I will lay it on the line — there is not one such fossil for which one could make a watertight argument. . . . It is easy to make up stories of how one form gave rise to another. . . . But such stories are not part of science, for there is no way of putting them to the test."[53]

One of the predictions made by Darwin regarding the theory of evolution was that no species would remain the same over a long period of time:[54] "We may safely infer that not one living species will transmit its unaltered likeness to a distant futurity."[55] But there are many examples of living organisms that have not changed at all from the time when some of their ancestors were fossilized. Consider the following examples:

- Bat fossils that are considered 50 million years old look essentially the same as today's bats of the same type.[56]

- Turtle fossils dated to 200 million years ago look virtually the same as today's turtles. "Turtles . . . have plodded a stolid and steady course through evolutionary time, changing very little in basic structure."[57]

- The famous broadcaster and writer David Attenborough described fossil sea pens, a type of jellyfish, in Australian rocks that are considered 650 million years old, and noted that sea pens are living in the sea less than 100 miles away.[58]

- The *coelacanth* is a bony fish that was known only from fossils dating back at least 65 million years, until a live specimen was caught in the Indian Ocean in 1938 — and many more have been discovered since. Live specimens are sold at Indonesian fish markets today.[59]

In many cases, it seems the controversy between creation and evolution is merely the result of each side's bias when interpreting the data. As evolutionist Stephen Jay Gould acknowledged, "We understand that biases, preferences, social values, and psychological attitudes all play a strong role in the process of discovery. . . . It is how we interpret these animals [in the fossil record], and what we say they mean for the history of life that is obviously subject to biased ways of thinking."[60]

APE-MAN

Australopithecus is one of the best-known ape-man fossil creatures. Evolutionists believe the creature walked upright and showed many characteristics intermediate between ape and man. The *Encyclopedia Britannica*, taking an evolutionary viewpoint, describes: "Many creatures intermediate between living apes and humans have been found as fossils.

Australopithecus, a hominid that lived 3,000,000 or 4,000,000 years ago, had an upright human stance but a cranial capacity of less than 500 cubic centimeters — comparable to that of a gorilla or chimpanzee and just about one-third that of humans. Its head displayed an odd mixture of ape and human characteristics: a low forehead and a long, ape-like face, but with teeth proportioned like those of humans."[61]

Although this view held by the *Encyclopedia* is prevalent amongst evolutionists, it has become significantly disputed by some experts, and thus cannot be held as undisputed evidence for human evolution. In fact, some prominent evolutionists themselves strongly doubt that *Australopithecus* was intermediate between ape and man.

Lord Solly Zuckerman, for many years the head of the department of anatomy at the University of Birmingham and chief scientific adviser to the British government, was knighted in 1964, awarded the Order of Merit in 1968, and elevated to a life peerage in 1971 in recognition of his distinguished career as a research scientist.[62] After more than 15 years of research on the subject, with a team that rarely included less than four scientists, Lord Zuckerman concluded that *Australopithecus* did not walk upright, and was not intermediate between ape and man, but was merely an anthropoid ape. Lord Zuckerman, although not a creationist, believed there was very little, if any, science in the search for man's fossil ancestry. Lord Zuckerman has written, based on a lifetime of investigation, that if man has evolved from an ape-like creature, he seemed to do so without leaving any trace of the transformation in the fossil record.[63]

"Lucy" is the popular name given to one of the most well-known australopithecine fossils ever found. American anthropologist Donald Johanson found this famous fossil skeleton in 1974 in Ethiopia. But according to Richard Leakey, who along with Johanson are probably the best-known fossil-anthropologists in the world, Lucy's skull is so incomplete that most of it is "imagination made of plaster," thus making it impossible to draw any firm conclusion about what species Lucy belonged to.[64]

Evolutionist Dr. Charles Oxnard (professor of anatomy and human biology at the University of Western Australia) completed one of the most sophisticated computer analyses of australopithecine fossils ever undertaken, and concluded that they have nothing to do with the ancestry of man, and are simply an extinct form of ape. "It is now recognized widely that the australopithecines are not structurally closely similar to humans."[65] Moreover, the world-renowned Richard Leakey has stated, "Biologists would dearly like to know how modern apes, modern humans, and the various ancestral hominids have evolved from a common ancestor. Unfortunately, the fossil record is somewhat incomplete as far as the hominids are concerned, and it is all but blank for the apes. . . . David Pilbeam (a well-known expert in human evolution) comments wryly, 'If you brought in a smart scientist from another discipline and showed him the meager evidence we've got he'd surely say, 'forget it: there isn't enough to go on.' "[66]

RADIO DATING

One need only look in virtually any reference text to quickly find that the earth is thought to be some 4.5 billion years old. As the *Encyclopedia Britannica* notes, methods such as measuring radioactive decay (radiometric dating) make it possible to estimate the time period when earth's rocks and associated fossils were formed.[67]

The most commonly used radiometric dating methods are potassium-argon, uranium-lead, and rubidium-strontium. The concept of how these methods work is simple: one element decays into another at a rather predictable rate. Potassium decays and becomes argon. Uranium decays into lead.

And rubidium decays into strontium. All three of these decay processes have half-lives measured in billions of years. Half-life is simply the time required for half of the atoms in a pound of uranium, for example, to disintegrate into lead.[68] That time is approximately 4.5 billion years.

The accuracy of these dating methods depends "critically" on several assumptions.[69] To date a rock by radiometric means, one must first assume:

1) What the initial amount of the parent atoms was at the time that the rock formed.

2) That the original composition of the rock contained no daughter atoms.[70]

3) That neither parent nor daughter atoms have ever been added or removed from the rock.

4) That the decay rate of parent atom to daughter atom has always remained constant.

If these assumptions are correct, then the radiometric dates are correct. However, there is no way to independently test these assumptions. If they are wrong, the method could yield faulty dates that might be far too old.

To illustrate, suppose there is a burning candle sitting on the table. How long has that candle been burning? This can be calculated if the candle's burn rate and original length is known. However, if the original length is not known, or if it cannot be verified that the burning rate has been constant, it is impossible to tell for sure how long the candle was burning. A similar problem occurs with radiometric dating of rocks. Since the initial physical state of the rock is unknowable, the age can only be estimated according to certain assumptions.

When dating a rock, the geochronologist (scientist who performs the dating procedure) must first assume the rock's age before it is dated. For example, if a scientist believes a piece of rock is 4.5 billion years old, he or she may then use the uranium-lead dating method because it has a half-life of about 4.5 billion years. This involves circular reasoning, as is clearly evident in the article on dating in the *Encyclopedia Britannica*: "Most geologists must rely on geochronologists for their results. In turn, the geochronologist relies on the geologist for relative ages."[71] The geochronologist must also be sure that the rate of decay, from uranium to lead for example, has remained constant in the rock over the past 4.5 billion years. Furthermore, the amount of uranium in the rock that was present to begin with must also be assumed. And neither uranium nor lead can have ever been added or removed from the specimen by any natural circumstances, catastrophic or otherwise. If all of these assumptions are correct, then the resulting dates are correct. However if even one of these assumptions is wrong, then the resulting dates are erroneous.

Why does radiometric dating repeatedly result in very old dates (such as billions of years)? While one explanation is that these dates show the specimens' true age, another is that one or more of these large assumptions associated with this method of dating is wrong.

Scientists have dated lava rock samples from various active volcanoes with the radiometric method. Because the formation of these rocks has recently been observed, radiometric dating should not give them an age of millions of years.[72] Yet there are many such examples. Consider the following:

- Rock which was formed in 1986 from a lava dome at Mount St. Helens volcano was dated by the potassium-argon method as 0.35 ± 0.05 million years old.[73]

- Rocks from five recent lava flows at Mount Ngauruhoe in New Zealand were dated using the potassium-argon method, and resulted in dates ranging from <0.27 to

3.5 million years — but one lava flow occurred in 1949, three in 1954, and one in 1975.[74]

- Salt Lake Crater on Oahu was determined to be 92–147 million years, 140–680 million years, 930–1,580 million years, 1,230–1,960 million years, 1,290–2,050 million years, and 1,360–1,900 years old, using different radiometric dating methods.[75]

- How did 1,000-year-old carbon-dated trees in the Auckland volcanic field of New Zealand get buried under 145,000-465,000 year old potassium-argon-dated lava rock?[76]

One explanation given by scientists for some of these incorrect dates is that excess argon was retained in the rocks when they solidified from a molten state. According to the *Canadian Journal of Earth Sciences*, "It is common to discard ages which are substantially too high or too low compared with the rest of the group or with other available data such as the geological time scale. . . . The discrepancies between the rejected and the accepted are arbitrarily attributed to excess or loss of argon."[77]

- But if excess argon can cause exaggerated dates for rocks of *known* age, then why should this dating method be trusted for rocks of *unknown* age?

No one knows for sure if any of the assumptions of radiometric dating are correct, however this is the only method of dating that is considered "absolute."[78] Physics professor and researcher Dr. Saami Shaibani, a leading consultant for America's Federal Bureau of Investigation (FBI), who has 100 scholarly articles to his credit and has been designated "international expert" in his field by the U.S. Departments of Labor and Justice, realizes, "In man-made dating methods, there is assumption upon assumption, plus a couple of more assumptions sprinkled in, plus some blind guesswork. And this masquerades as wonderful, legitimate methodology, but it's not."[79]

Creationist scientists distrust the radiometric method of dating, reasoning that 90 percent of the methods that have been used to estimate the age of the earth give far younger ages than those of radiometric dating.[80] "The age of our globe is presently thought to be some 4.5 billion years, based on [radiometric dating]. Such 'confirmation' may be short-lived, as nature is not to be discovered quite so easily. There has been in recent years the horrible realization that radio-decay rates are not as constant as previously thought, nor are they immune to environmental influences. And this could mean that the atomic clocks are reset during some global disaster, and events which brought the Mesozoic [the dinosaur age] to a close may not be 65 million years ago, but rather, within the age and memory of man."[81]

STARLIGHT

Some stars are millions — even billions — of light-years away. Since a light-year is the distance traveled by light in one year, doesn't this mean that the light now received from such a star has taken millions of years to get here? How could light possibly get to earth, it is asked, from stars which are billions of light years away, unless the universe is at least billions of years old?

Recently, a top creationist scientist, physicist Dr. Russell Humphreys, winner of several scientific awards, has presented an interesting possibility.[82] He points out that the real question is "how far away were the galaxies when the light started out on its trip to us?" Dr. Humphreys has found a solution to Einstein's gravitational field equations which may allow a very rapid expansion of space and all things in it.[83] Thus, the starlight would have begun its journey when galaxies were much closer (and also much smaller and less energetic) than today. This is a rather different theory than the popular "big-bang" cosmology; it raises the mathematical possibility that the universe inflated to its present size in only thousands of years, contrasted with the traditional billions of years commonly believed.[84]

Educational science textbooks sometimes note that origins theories such as the big bang are based largely on speculation, and as such may have their flaws. Dr. Keith Wanser, professor of physics at California State University, affirms that the confident public image of the "certainty" of the latest physical theories, including big-bang cosmology, is a far cry from reality. "The sad thing is that the public is so overawed by these things, just because there is complex maths involved. They don't realize how much philosophical speculation and imagination is injected along with the maths — these are really stories that are made up." Furthermore, he says, "People look at the sort of science that put men on the moon, and they put these 'big-bang' theories in the same basket. They're unaware of all the speculation and uncertainty (even rule-bending) there is in physical theories of origins."[85] Dr. Wanser's primary field of interest is experimental and theoretical condensed matter physics; he has authored about 50 published scientific papers, and also holds seven U.S. patents.

THE CREATION MODEL

The biblical Book of Genesis describes a great cataclysmic flood that supposedly covered the entire earth approximately 4,500 years ago.[86] Famously known as the story of Noah's ark, this flood was to destroy every living creature on earth except one man named Noah, his wife, their sons and their son's wives, seven pairs of each animal that was approved by God for eating and sacrificing, seven pairs of every kind of bird, and one pair of every other kind of animal, male and female; all these were saved in a large boat (or ark).

While evolutionists dismiss this biblical account as plainly mythical, most creationist scientists see it as a literal historical fact. In fact, a literal interpretation of this account is central to the creation model. Yet, if this biblical account is to be taken seriously, it must be demonstrated that the story is not unreasonable to believe as an actual fact of history. If such a worldwide flood occurred sometime in the past, the account should stand up to an objective analysis; not only must it be reasonable, there should also be evidence to support its claims.[87]

Recall that the best and most likely way for a fossil to be produced is by the rapid burial of a creature at the time of its death. A worldwide flood, then, would be a good explanation of how most of the fossils around the globe could have been produced. Millions of living creatures all over the earth would have naturally been quickly killed, buried, and fossilized in such a great cataclysm.

Thus, if the biblical account of a global flood and its aftermath is true, one would not only expect to find sedimentary layers (rocks laid down by water) all over the earth, but one would also expect these rocks to contain the fossil remains of many kinds of creatures. Where there are similar types of creatures alive today, these fossils would be basically the same as their living representatives — for example, bats would still look like bats, and turtles like turtles.

Indeed, these predictions are observed to be fulfilled. Today most of the earth's surface (80 to 90 percent) is in fact composed of sedimentary rock,[88] consistent with the expected results of a biblical global flood. And many fossils highly resemble today's creatures — that is, fossil bats look like today's bats, and fossil turtles like today's turtles.

Additionally, many types of animals that lived before the Flood would have died out. Many marine creatures, for example, would have died out during the Flood, and many land creatures would also have become extinct during the succeeding centuries. Thus, one would predict that many creatures would be found in the fossil record that look quite unrelated to anything alive today. Again, that is exactly what is found. For instance, the pterosaurs (flying reptiles), as well as the dinosaurs and many other extinct types of animals can be observed in the fossil record, but are not living today.

Noah's Ark

How could the ark described above have possibly carried all the different types of animals?

The Genesis "kind" of animal is undoubtedly a more flexible term than the biological *species*. Many of today's species of animals could have descended from these different "kinds." Thus, if the scientific *genus* is taken to be equal to the biblical "kind,"[89] then this would result in about 8,000 genera, and therefore, nearly 16,000 animals on the ark (this accounts for both live animals and extinct animals known from fossils).[90]

Noah would not have needed to take sea creatures because they would not necessarily be threatened with extinction by a flood. However, turbulent water would cause massive carnage, as seen in the fossil record, and many oceanic species probably would have become extinct because of the Flood. Noah would not have needed to take plants either — many could have survived as seeds, and others could have survived on floating mats of vegetation. Many insects and other invertebrates were small enough to have survived on these mats as well.[91] The ark had to transport only land animals, so the mammals, birds, and reptiles were essentially all that would have needed accommodations.

There would have been ample space available on the ark to store these animals. According to the biblical record, the ark measured about 137x23x14 meters or 450x75x45 feet,[92] so its volume was about 44,000 m^3 or 1.5 million cubic feet.

To put this in perspective, this is the equivalent volume of about 522 standard American railroad stock cars, each of which can hold about 240 sheep. So the ark could have carried over 125,000 fully-grown sheep. The animals, however, did not have to be fully grown. The largest animals could have been represented by "teenage" or even younger specimens. The average size of the animals on the ark could actually have been that of a small rat, according to up-to-date tabulations, while only about 11 percent may have been much larger than a sheep.[93]

According to the biblical account, the ark was constructed in three stories, and each was fitted with "rooms" or "nests" — evidently tiers of cages or stalls — to store the different kinds of animals (Gen. 6:14). If the animals were kept in cages with an average size of about 20x20x12 inches, i.e., 4,800 cubic inches, then 16,000 animals would occupy only 42,000 cubic feet, or about 14 of 522 railroad stock cars. However, even assuming the average size of the animals to be that of fully-grown sheep rather than that of small rats, they would occupy only about 15 percent of the available ark space (i.e., 75 of 522 available railroad stock cars). Thus, there would have been ample room for food storage and living quarters for Noah and his family.

Although there also would have been plenty of room for the animals to get exercise, once they were safely on board, lodged in their stalls, and properly fed, many of the animals could have settled down for a long period of dormancy, or hibernation.

Post-Flood Animal Migration

A common objection that is often raised is, "Following the flood, how did animals get from the ark to isolated places, such as Australia?" However, evolutionary anthropologists themselves have no difficulty in acknowledging that men and animals were once freely able to cross the Bering Strait, which separates Asia and the Americas. In fact, before the idea of continental drift became popular, evolutionists taught and believed that a lowering of the sea level in the past would mean that there were land bridges enabling dry-land passage from Europe most of the way to Australia, for example. The existence of some deep-water stretches along this route is consistent with this explanation; evolutionary geologists themselves believe there have been major tectonic upheavals, accompanied by substantial rising and falling of sea-floors, in the time-period associated with the Ice Age.[94] This would have made it possible for animals to migrate over land or ice bridges for centuries.

In fact, there is a widespread, but mistaken, belief that marsupials (such as kangaroos) are found only in Australia. But live marsupials are found also in the Americas, and fossil marsupials on every continent. Likewise, monotremes, such as the platypus, were once thought to be unique to Australia, but the recent discovery of a platypus fossil in South America stunned the scientific community![95] Therefore, even in evolutionary terms, since marsupials are all believed to have come from a common ancestor, migration between Australia and other areas *must* have been possible.

Racial Diversity

Succeeding the biblical worldwide flood story, it follows that all humans on earth today would be descended from a group of eight people: Noah, his wife, his three sons, and their wives. Because today there are obvious differences between "races" (i.e., skin color), many believe that a literal interpretation of the biblical record must be impossible; such diversity could only have arisen by evolving separately over tens of thousands of years.

Modern genetics show, however, that when a large freely interbreeding group is suddenly broken into many smaller groups which from then on breed only among themselves, different racial characteristics will arise very rapidly. A simple lesson in heredity shows that one pair of middle-brown colored parents could produce children of all known shades of color, from very light to very dark, in just *one* generation.

The biblical record contends that for several centuries there was only one language and one culture group in the world. If so, this would mean there would be no barriers to marriage within this group, which would tend to keep the skin color of the population away from the extremes. Very dark and very light skin would appear, of course, but people tending in either direction would be free to marry someone less dark or less light than themselves, ensuring that the average color stayed roughly the same. Under these circumstances, distinct racial lines would never emerge. This is true for animals as well as human populations. To obtain separate racial lines, one would need to break a large breeding group into smaller groups and keep them separate, that is, not interbreeding any more.

If the Bible is taken literally regarding its claim that the "whole world spoke a single language" and that God subsequently confused mankind by supernaturally "giving them many languages, thus scattering them across the earth,"[96] people would have consequently begun to break up into smaller breeding groups. Once separate languages were imposed, there would have been instantaneous barriers. Not only would people tend not to marry someone they couldn't understand, but entire groups which spoke the same language would have difficulty relating to and trusting those who did not speak the same language. Thus, humanity would have been broken into smaller "breeding" groups, and would therefore begin to develop distinguishing "racial" characteristics in a very short period of time.

DINOSAURS

Without a doubt, dinosaur fossils tell of the great variety and large numbers in which the giant creatures once existed. Gigantic fossil remains have revealed the awe-inspiring size to which some of the dinosaur species grew. Often, one cannot help feeling a sense of mystery about the total absence of dinosaurs today, leading to the question, "What caused the extinction of the dinosaurs?"

The prevailing evolutionary explanation for why dinosaurs disappeared is that the impact from a massive meteorite threw up so much dust that the skies darkened, causing the climate to cool and the vegetation sustaining the giant, cold-blooded herbivores to die. Then, with widespread starvation among the herbivores, carnivores were left without adequate prey on which to survive.

However, one evolutionary book on dinosaurs explains the many problems associated with such dinosaur extinction theories: "Now comes the important question. What caused all these extinctions [of dinosaurs and other animals] at one particular point in [history]? Dozens of reasons have been suggested, some serious and sensible, others quite crazy, and yet others merely as a joke. Every year people come up with new theories on this thorny problem. The trouble is that if we are to find just one reason to account for them all, it would have to explain the death, all at the same time, of animals living on land and of animals living in the sea; but, in both cases, of only some of those animals, for many of the land-dwellers and many of the sea-dwellers went on living quite happily into the following period. Alas, no such one explanation exists."[97]

But one such explanation *does* exist, according to creationist scientists. Like evolutionists, creationists believe that the dinosaurs became extinct as a consequence of some major catastrophe. But while most evolutionists believe this catastrophe may have been a colossal meteor collision with earth, creationists believe it to be the cataclysmic, worldwide deluge known as the Genesis flood.

A recent discovery of thousands of fossilized dinosaur eggs shows that dinosaur eggs were only about the size of little grapefruits (including species which grew up to 50 feet long).[98] So from a creationist perspective, very young (thus very small) dinosaurs could have been taken aboard Noah's ark with ample room to spare, but not have survived as long in the new environment following the Genesis flood. (Interestingly, it is acknowledged by evolutionists that the eggs were rapidly buried in silt from a flood.[99])

After the Flood, the land animals that survived on the ark would have found their new world to be much different than the one before. Due to (1) competition for food that was no longer in abundance, (2) the destruction of habitats, (3) man hunting for food, and (4) other catastrophes, many species of animals would have continued to eventually die out even after the Flood. Today numerous animal species become extinct every year — extinction seems to be the rule in earth history.[100] Thus, the group of animals now called dinosaurs could have simply died out in addition to the other animals that became extinct after the Flood.

As described in the previous section, many sea creatures would have died out during the Genesis flood, but some would have survived. In addition, all of the land animals outside of the ark would have died, but the representatives of many of the kinds that survived on the ark would have continued to live in the new world after the Flood. Indeed, these points alone explain satisfactorily, as noted above, "the death, all at the same time, of animals living on land and of animals living in the sea; but, in both cases, of only some of those animals."

It can thus be seen that although evolutionists believe "no such one explanation exists," they probably have not considered the creation model, which can satisfactorily explain the observed data surrounding the extinction of the dinosaurs and other animals.

Is there a dinosaur/dragon relationship? Clearly, it seems far-fetched, at first, to imagine dinosaurs living alongside mankind. After all, Hollywood films such as *Jurassic Park* portray dinosaurs as vicious predators who ruled the earth. But, actually, even evolutionists believe that most dinosaurs were not the vicious predators often pictured, but rather, just vegetarians or scavengers! In fact, the *American Museum of Natural History* acknowledges that, based on the evidence to date, meat-eating dinosaurs such as *T. rex*, the most famous of all fearsome dinosaurs, may not have been the ferocious predators often imagined: "While the *Tyrannosaurus rex* is posed as if it is stalking prey, we do not in fact know for sure whether meat-eating dinosaurs such as this were active hunters — tracking down, attacking, and killing prey — or scavengers, feeding on the carcasses of other dinosaurs."[101] Significantly, many animals today that might *look* like vicious killers are often not.[102]

Since it is known that dinosaurs indeed lived alongside other mammals in the past, there is no reason to assume that dinosaurs could not have been contemporaries with mankind as well.[103] Stories abound of ancient legends of dragons, sea serpents, and monsters, such as the Beowulf epic, and St. George and the Dragon. Tales of enormous fire-breathing monsters can be found in diverse parts of the world. Interestingly, ancient depictions of these dragons tend to exhibit one recurring observation: they bear a remarkable resemblance to today's dinosaur fossil reconstructions. Indeed, the article on dragons in the 1949 edition of *Encyclopedia Britannica* noted that dinosaurs are "astonishingly dragon-like." The most recent edition of the *Encyclopedia* notes that the belief in dragons "apparently arose without the slightest knowledge on the part of the ancients of the gigantic, prehistoric, dragon-like reptiles [dinosaurs]."[104]

It may simply be a coincidence that, before dinosaur bones were discovered about 150 years ago, ancient people depicted creatures which highly resemble today's fossil dinosaur reconstructions. But is it necessarily a coincidence? Is it possible that such drawings and stories have a basis in real past encounters with dinosaurs, suggesting that at least some dinosaurs might have been contemporaries with mankind in the past? Even the biblical Book of Job describes some creatures whose descriptions strongly resemble a dinosaur (Job 40:15–24; Job 41). Scholars have suggested that Job may be the oldest book of the Bible; perhaps he was an eyewitness to these animals. This is one of the very few animals in the Bible that is singled out for such a detailed description, suggesting that Job knew what this animal looked like and lived alongside it.

Breathing Fire

That large dragon-like creatures (dinosaurs) once roamed the earth is certainly evidenced by the fossil record. But breathing fire? Surely preposterous. Even if dragon stories do have basis in real past encounters with dinosaurs, it is likely these accounts have also accumulated some mythical elements over the centuries, such as breathing fire. But consider these bizarre facts:

> Some dinosaurs (specifically the Lambeo-saurus) are particularly notable for the hatchet-shaped hollow bony crest on top of their skulls. The *Encyclopedia Britannica* describes this crest as containing "complex chamber extensions of the breathing passage between the nostrils and the [main tube by which air enters the lungs]." The article notes that "the function of these chambers is not known," although various uses have been suggested.[105]

One possibility is that these complex breathing chambers may have been similar in concept to the reaction chamber of an insect called the *bombardier beetle*. This little beetle is endowed with an ability to imitate exploding gunpowder. Little sacs at the tip of its abdomen spray a noxious fluid at boiling-hot temperatures. The fluid itself consists of toxins called quinones that react explosively (at an estimated rate of 500 bursts per second) in an internal "combustion" chamber with hydrogen peroxide, which is also produced by the beetle and stored in a separate body compartment.[106]

With complex chambers in their breathing passages, could certain dinosaurs have had the same kind of defense system operating from their heads as the bombardier beetle (i.e., some type of fire-breathing capabilities)? To date, there has been no other definitive explanation for these dinosaurs' strange head-crest chambers.

ODDS & COMPLEXITY

In the biological world of living things lie the most complex concepts of engineering known to mankind. The *Encyclopedia Britannica* concedes, "A living cell is a marvel of detailed and complex architecture. . . . The information content of a simple cell has been estimated as around 10^{12} bits, comparable to about one hundred million pages of *Encyclopedia Britannica*."[107] The human body comprises a conglomeration of some 100,000,000,000,000 (10^{14}) cells which work together in perfect harmony to maintain human life.[108]

It has become very common to speak of evolution from a single-cell to a human, as if the cell was the simple beginning of the process. On the contrary, if life arose from nonliving matter, the progression from dead matter to a single cell was at least as great as from a single cell to a human. The most elementary type of living cell constitutes precise engineering that is unimaginably more complex than any machine yet thought up, let alone constructed, by mankind. Molecular biologist Dr. Michael Denton explains what is involved:

> To grasp the reality of life as it has been revealed by molecular biology, we must magnify a cell a thousand million times until it is twenty kilometers in diameter and resembles a giant airship large enough to cover a great city like London or New York. What we would then see would be an object of unparalleled complexity and adaptive design. On the surface of the cell we would see millions of openings, like the portholes of a vast spaceship, opening and closing to allow a continual stream of materials to flow in and out. If we were to enter one of these openings we would find ourselves in a world of supreme technology and bewildering complexity.[109]

If a living cell is compared to a computer, the cell's DNA might be considered equivalent to computer software, and the cell itself (which contains the DNA) would be equivalent to computer hardware. Just as a computer software program (code) determines what the computer will do, so a cell's DNA code determines what the cell will do. The DNA code is four digits, error correcting, overlapping, and self-replicating. It would be the equivalent of a computer software program that could fix its own errors and reproduce both itself and the computer it resides in.

The amount of DNA information that can be stored in a space the size of a pinhead is equivalent to the information content of a pile of paperback books 500 times as tall as the distance from earth to the moon. Indeed, living things have by far the most compact information storage/retrieval system known to mankind.

Creationist scientists (and now a growing number of non-creationist scientists as well) believe that the DNA molecule, which is billions of times more complex than the most powerful computer to date, did not spontaneously form by itself, but was intelligently created by a Master Designer.

Dr. Denton asks:

Is it really credible that random processes could have constructed a reality, the smallest element of which — a functional protein or gene — is complex beyond our own creative capacities, a reality which is the very antithesis of chance, which excels in every sense anything produced by the intelligence of man? Alongside the level of ingenuity and complexity exhibited by the molecular machinery of life, even our most advanced artifacts appear clumsy.[110]

What are the Odds?

The mathematical probabilities against the spontaneous generation of life are sometimes acknowledged by evolutionists as a strong argument for creation. The odds in favor of the chance formation of a functional simple cell are acknowledged to be worse than 1 in $10^{40,000}$.[111] The scientist Sir Frederick Hoyle, a renowned mathematician from Cambridge known for many popular science works,[112] has used analogies to try to convey the immensity of the problem. For a more graspable notion of the improbability, he has calculated the odds of the accidental formation of a simple living cell to be roughly comparable to the odds of rolling double-sixes 50,000 times in a row with unloaded dice.[113]

As another comparison, Hoyle asks, what are the chances that a tornado might blow through a junkyard containing all the parts of a 747 and just accidentally assemble it so as to leave it sitting there all set for take-off? "So small as to be negligible," Hoyle says, "even if a tornado were to blow through enough junkyards to fill the whole universe."[114] Although not a creationist, Hoyle's calculations have convinced him that there must have been some "intelligence" behind the emergence of life on earth.

Likewise, Nobel Prize winner Dr. Francis Crick also arrived at the theory that life could never have evolved by chance on planet Earth.[115] Because he is a co-discoverer of the molecular structure of DNA, an accomplishment which became a cornerstone of genetics and which is widely regarded as one of the most important discoveries of 20th century biology,[116] his conclusion is particularly noteworthy — especially since he is an atheist!

Why would these (and many other) distinguished scientists come to such conclusions? For a clearer perspective, consider the following "coin-toss" analogy: Suppose I announce that I am going to repeatedly flip a coin and hope to come up with a sequence of all heads. So I proceed to flip the coin, and it comes up heads. You say, "Okay." I flip it a second time, and it comes up heads again. You say, "Okay." I flip it again, and it comes up heads again. You say "Hmmm, okay." Say I flip it again, and it comes up heads a fourth time. You say "Hmmm." Say I flip it again, and it comes up heads a fifth time. You say "Wait a minute, what's going on here?" I flip it again, and it comes up heads a sixth time. You say "Stop, this isn't fair." I say, "Why?" You say, "It isn't random. You're doing something to make that coin come up heads each time." I flip it again, and it comes up heads a seventh time. I say, "Look, millions of people have flipped coins throughout history. This was bound to happen sooner or later." I flip it again, and it comes up heads an eighth time. You say, "Come on, what are you doing?" I flip it again, and it comes up heads a ninth time. I say, "Nothing. Really! I'm just flipping this coin and it keeps coming up heads by chance." I flip it again, and it comes up heads a tenth time. You say, "You're a liar. What do you take me for, some sort of fool?"

Now, if it is true that over a million people have tossed coins throughout history then maybe you should have waited until at least 20 throws (since 2^{20} is over a million) before considering crying "foul." But most people, in fact, won't. Why did the observer in the above example not wait that long? Because after 10 tries she concluded that she could call the coin-thrower a liar based on the non-random results. Statistically, she would have only one chance in a thousand (1 in 2^{10}) of being wrong!

Given the lower probabilities of the origin-of-life issue, it is thus consistent to conclude that life did not spontaneously originate by chance. A person who comes to such a conclusion would have less than a 1 in $10^{40,000}$ (that's 10 followed by 40,000 zeros) chance of being wrong, solely on the basis of mathematical probabilities. In any case, this person is not to be taken for some sort of fool.

CHANCE DESIGN?

A growing number of scientists, both creationists and non-creationists alike, are beginning to argue that not only is life complex, but also that it is ordered in such a way as to exhibit evidence of intelligent design. Since life is at its core a chemical code (the DNA code), the origin of life is thus the origin of a code. A code is a very special kind of order — it represents "specified complexity" (high information content).[117]

In everyday experience, people detect intelligent design all the time. For example, if a school teacher finds a sequence of lettered building blocks on the floor of a kindergarten classroom which spells out THESE BLOCKS WERE NOT PUT HERE ON PURPOSE, the teacher can safely assume that someone did arrange the letters in that order on purpose — no one would suppose they accidentally fell down that way. This arrangement of building blocks shows specified complexity (i.e., it contains meaningful information).

The meaningful arrangement of bases (or "letters") in the DNA code of living things is far higher in information content than that of the arrangement of kindergarten building blocks. Indeed, the *Encyclopedia Britannica* concedes that the information content of a single simple cell is encyclopedic — comparable to about one hundred million pages of *Encyclopedia Britannica*. Thus, if it is unreasonable to believe that the arrangement of kindergarten building blocks could have originated without intelligence, then it is at least as unreasonable to believe that the encyclopedic amounts of information contained in the DNA code could have originated without intelligence.

Everyday experience reveals that information is only produced with intelligence; it always takes an intelligent agent to generate information. In nature, there is no example anywhere in which meaningful information has been observed to arise by itself, without an intelligent source.[118]

The Search for Extra-terrestrial Intelligence (SETI) would be pointless if there was no criterion for determining what constitutes an intelligent source. The criterion for SETI is a radio signal from outer space with a high level of specified complexity — a signal like this would prove that there was some kind of an intelligent sender.[119]

If specified complexity indicates an intelligent source for SETI, then why shouldn't the high specified complexity found in the DNA of living things, equivalent to millions of pages of *Encyclopedia Britannica*, also indicate an intelligent source?

Today it is becoming clearer that the biblical creation model is *not unreasonable* to believe as a fact of history. The creation model stands up to an objective analysis; it is consistent with what is observed around the earth today.[120]

The more that is discovered about the detailed and complex architecture of living things, the stronger the evidence seems to become for the involvement of a Master Designer. It is for precisely this reason that many famed scientists, such as the co-discoverer of DNA, who made one of the most important scientific discoveries of the 20th century, have begun to abandon their faith in chance alone.

Footnotes

1 Specifically, the Kansas State Board of Education, new Science Education Standards, as of August 11, 1999, banned the testing of "*macro-evolution*," a decision which ignited so much controversy by evolutionists, that most of the supporting board members were later voted off, allowing the possibility for the decision to be reversed.

2 A great portion of the material in this chapter has been provided by the creation-based organization, *Answers in Genesis Ministries International*, <http://www.answersingenesis.org>. Some material has also been taken from the book *Refuting Evolution* by Jonathan Sarfati (Green Forest, AR: Master Books, 1999).

3 "Darwin's Death in South Kensington," *Nature*, February 26, 1981, p. 735.

4 *Nature*, vol. 290, March 12, 1981, p. 82.

5 "Theodosius Dobzhansky," Encyclopedia Britannica Online, <http://members.eb.com/bol/topic?eu=31253&sctn=1>

6 T. Dobzhansky, *Evolution*, vol. 29, 1975, p. 376–378.

7 Pierre Grassé, *Evolution du Vivant* (New York, NY: Academic Press, 1977).

8 Professor Louis Bounoure as quoted in *The Advocate*, March 8, 1984, p. 17.

9 "Louis Pasteur," Encyclopedia Britannica Online, <http://members.eb.com/bol/topic?eu=114943&sctn=1>

10 "The Death of Spontaneous Generation," Encyclopedia Britannica Online, <http://members.eb.com/bol/topic?eu=119731&sctn=29>

11 Dr. Michael Behe caused a stir in the scientific community by elaborating these ideas in *Darwin's Black Box* (New York, NY: Free Press, 1996).

12 The article reads, "Due to a rapid and efficient photochemical consumption of CH4 and NH3, a methane-ammonia atmosphere would have a maximum lifetime of about 1,000,000 years. This finding is of interest because it has been suggested that life originated from mixtures of organic compounds synthesized by nonbiological reactions starting from methane and ammonia. Recognition of the short atmospheric lifetimes of these materials poses grave difficulties for such a theory." ("Atmosphere: Photochemical Reactions," Encyclopedia Britannica Online, <http://members.eb.com/bol/topic?eu=118221&sctn=9>)

13 J. Levine, *New Ideas about the Early Atmosphere*, NASA Special Report, No. 225, Langley Research Center, August 11, 1983.

14 For a deeper analysis of the spontaneous generation or "chemical evolution" issue, visit the Answers in Genesis website at <http://www.answersingenesis.org/home/area/faq/origin.asp>

15 George Wald, "The Origin of Life," *Scientific American*, August, 1954. In the remainder of his article, Wald goes on to argue that perhaps the impossible is not so impossible after all. Like many evolutionists, he asserts that given enough time, anything might be possible, and thus argues that spontaneous generation is possible. But *time* itself is not creative. In fact, the scientific law of entropy indicates the very opposite. For example, a shiny new metal sword left in the forest would rust and break down over time — it would not organize itself into a more complicated structure. Just because enough time goes by does not mean that the impossible can become possible. Experience suggests the very opposite in the natural world. See "Thermodynamics vs. Evolutionism, How Do Creationists Respond to Evolutionists' Counter-arguments, e.g., Open Systems and Crystals?" Timothy Wallace, <http://www.trueorigin.org/steiger.htm>.

16 "Evolution," Encyclopedia Britannica Online, <http://members.eb.com/bol/topic?eu=108620&sctn=6>

17 "If the sequence [of the DNA code] is changed at random, the 'meaning' rarely will be improved and often will be hampered or destroyed." ("Evolution," Encyclopedia Britannica Online, <http://members.eb.com/bol/topic?eu=108620&sctn=6>)

18 "Mutation," Encyclopedia Britannica Online, <http://members.eb.com/bol/topic?eu=55860&sctn=1> Other mutations may be neutral; that is, not damaging enough to cause any major consequences.

19 Neil A. Campbell, *Biology*, 4th Edition (Menlo Park, CA: University of California, The Benjamin/Cummings Publishing Company, Inc., 1996).

20 "Mutation," Encyclopedia Britannica Online, <http://members.eb.com/bol/topic?eu=55860&sctn=1>

21 See "Philosophy of Nature," Encyclopedia Britannica Online, <http://members.eb.com/bol/topic?eu=115092&sctn=19>

22 "Information" itself is not tangible — it transcends chemistry and physics. The material base of a message is completely independent of the information transmitted. The content of the sentence "Apples are sweet" does not change when it is written in crayon instead of ink. It is unaffected by a switch to chalk or pencil. The same thing can be said if it is written in the sand. It can even be translated into the dots and dashes of Morse code. The information transmitted by the writing is not within the ink used to write it. Likewise, the information within the genetic code is entirely independent of the chemical makeup of the DNA molecule. The information transmitted by the sequence of bases has nothing to do with the bases themselves. There is nothing in the chemicals themselves that originates the communication transmitted to the cell by the DNA molecule. For a long time, biologists overlooked the distinction between two kinds of order (simple, periodic order versus specified complexity). Only recently have the leading origin-of-life researchers appreciated that the distinguishing feature of living systems is not order but specified complexity (information). (Source: "DNA, Design, and the Origin of Life," article by Charles B. Thaxton, <http://www.leaderu.com/science/thaxton_dna.html>)

23 This is true even if the production of the wings occurs in small, gradual steps. Biochemist Michael Behe, in his book *Darwin's Black Box*, explains that many structures in living things show irreducible complexity, far in excess of any man-made machine. In other words, the complexity of a structure cannot be reduced without destroying its function entirely, thus making the gradual production of such a structure practically unfeasible by strictly natural processes.

24 National Academy of Sciences Staff, *Teaching About Evolution and the Nature of Science* (Washington, DC: National Academy of Sciences Staff, 1998), p. 16–17.

25 One example is resistance to the antibiotic penicillin. Bacteria normally produce an enzyme, penicillinase, which destroys penicillin. The amount of penicillinase is controlled by a gene. There is normally enough produced to handle any penicillin encountered in the "wild,"

but the bacteria is overwhelmed by the amount given to patients. A mutation disabling this controlling gene results in much more penicillinase being produced. This enables the bacterium to resist the antibiotic. See the book *Refuting Evolution* by Jonathan Sarfati (Green Forest, AR: Master Books, 1999) for more info and references.

26 Reuters News Service, April 23, 1998.

27 Including Canada's Royal Ontario Museum.

28 In fact, it is now widely accepted that the entire story of the peppered moths was false and involved fraud. See *Journal of Animal Ecology*, vol. 44, 1975, p. 67–83; also *Nature*, vol. 396, p.35–36; also *Washington Times*, January 17, 1999, p. D8.

29 "Evolution," Encyclopedia Britannica Online, <http://members.eb.com/bol/topic?eu=108620&sctn=6>

30 *From a Frog to a Prince*, video distributed by Answers in Genesis (AiG) organization. Some skeptics have accused AiG of fraudulently doctoring the video, however AiG denies such charges and has forwarded the original recording of events to anti-creationist sources who, in one particular instance, reversed their charge after listening to the recording.

31 *Creation ex nihilo* magazine, September–November 1998. Dawkins has since written an essay in response to this question, but in it he still has not pointed to any specific example. Creationist scientists have also written a rebuttal to this essay, which is available online at <http://www.trueorigins.org/dawkinfo.htm>.

32 *Creation ex nihilo* magazine, March–May 1999.

33 "Stephen Jay Gould," Encyclopedia Britannica Online, <http://members.eb.com/bol/topic?eu=38285&sctn=1>; also *Science* magazine, vol. 279, 1998.

34 S.J. Gould, "Is a New and General Theory of Evolution Emerging?" *Paleobiology Journal*, vol. 6, 1980, p. 119–130, reprinted in the collection by John Maynard Smith, *Evolution Now: A Century after Darwin* (San Francisco, CA: Freeman, 1982). Gould himself believed in evolution, but developed his own theory to explain it (which, to date, has not been widely accepted among evolutionists).

35 Dr. Carl Wieland, "Beetle Bloopers," <http://www.answersingenesis.org/docs/241.asp>

36 "Fossil," Encyclopedia Britannica Online, <http://members.eb.com/bol/topic?eu=35639&sctn=1>

37 This quote, and most of the foregoing paragraph, is from "Evolution," Encyclopedia Britannica Online, <http://members.eb.com/bol/topic?eu=108619&sctn=9>.

38 *Science*, January 14, 1994.

39 *Science*, vol. 274, 1996.

40 *New Scientist*, vol. 154, April 12, 1997.

41 *Time*, Australia, April 26, 1993.

42 *Major Features of Vertebrate Evolution*, convened by Donald R. Prothero and Robert M. Schoch, "On the Origin of Birds and of Avian Flight" by John H. Ostrom (Knoxville, TN: Paleontological society, 1994).

   Much of the information in the foregoing two paragraphs is from Jonathan Sarfati, *Refuting Evolution* (Green Forest, AR: Master Books, 1999), p. 60, 73.

43 "Turtle," Encyclopedia Britannica Online, <http://members.eb.com/bol/topic?eu=118989&sctn=5>. Emphasis added.

44 Ibid. Emphasis added.

45 "Conflicts Between Darwin and Paleontology," Raup, Field Museum of Natural History Bulletin, January 1979, p. 22–26.

   Note: This text deals only with intermediary stages between *major transitions* in organic design. A discussion of the appearance in the fossil record of what is known as "faunal [fossil] succession" (i.e., the notion that least complex fossils progressively become more complex in each rock layer upwards in the geologic column) lies outside the scope of this text — but see reference at end of this footnote. It should be noted, however, that the global "stack" of index fossils actually exists nowhere on earth, and most index fossils do not usually overlie each other at the same locality, as commonly believed. In fact, only a small fraction of index fossils are superposed at the same location on earth. (These facts are fully documented in the reference at the end of this footnote.) As for the degree to which faunal succession is actually apparent in the geologic column, the "creation model" adequately explains it (however still outside the scope of this book — but see reference). Such explanations include mechanisms such as the sorting of organisms during the Flood, differential escape of organisms during the same, ecological zonation of life-forms in the antediluvian world (such that different life-forms in different strata reflect the serial burial of ecological life-zones during the Flood), and TABs (Tectonically-Associated Biological Provinces — wherein different life forms occur in successive horizons of rock as a reflection of successive crustal downwarp of different life-bearing biogeographic communities). See John Woodmorappe, *Studies in Flood Geology*, 2nd Edition (El Cajon, CA: Institute for Creation Research, 1999).

46 S.J. Gould, *Natural History*, June–July 1976, May 1977; S.J. Gould, "The Ediacaran Experiment," *Natural History*, 93(2):14-23, February

1984. While natural selection may account for *minor* changes in creatures observed in the fossil record (which no one contests), Gould clearly acknowledged that "the absence of fossil evidence for intermediary stages between *major transitions* in organic design . . . has been a persistent and nagging problem for gradualistic accounts of evolution." This statement eliminates any false accusations of misquoting in this context. Smith, *Evolution Now: A Century After Darwin,* p.140; emphasis added.

47 Charles Darwin, *Origin of Species* (New York, NY: E.P. Dutton, 1972).

48 In 1972, Eldredge and Gould together developed the theory of punctuated equilibria.

49 Niles Eldredge, *The Myths of Human Evolution* (New York, NY: Columbia University Press, 1982), p. 45–46.

50 "Conflicts Between Darwin and Paleontology," Raup, Field Museum of Natural History Bulletin, January 1979, p. 22–26.

51 Luther D. Sunderland, *Darwin's Enigma*, 4th edition (Green Forest, AR: 1988), p. 78, quoting Niles Eldredge.

52 Patterson has made important contributions to paleontology (*Encyclopedia Britannica*).

53 Sunderland, *Darwin's Enigma*, p. 89.

54 "A long period of time" in this context is presumably millions of years.

55 Darwin, *Origin of Species*.

56 The University of California, Berkeley, Museum of Paleontology, <http://www.ucmp.berkeley.edu/mammal/eutheria/chirofr.html>

57 "Turtle," Encyclopedia Britannica Online, <http://members.eb.com/bol/topic?eu=118989&sctn=5>

58 David Attenborough, *Life on Earth* (Boston, MA: Little, Brown, 1979), p. 32.

59 *Cincinnati Enquirer,* November 14, 1998, p. B6.

60 *Stanford Daily*, November 4, 1998; also *Time* magazine, May 14, 1990.

61 "Evolution," Encyclopedia Britannica Online, <http://members.eb.com/bol/topic?eu=108619&sctn=9>

62 "Lord Solly Zuckerman," Encyclopedia Britannica Online, <http://members.eb.com/bol/topic?eu=123749&sctn=1>

63 Solly Zuckerman, *Beyond the Ivory Tower* (London: Weidenfeld & Nicolson, 1970), p.64; also *Journal of the Royal College of Surgeons of Edinburgh*, Vol. 11, 1966, p. 87–115. The full quote reads as follows: "No scientist could logically dispute the proposition that man, without having been involved in any act of divine creation, evolved from some ape-like creature in a very short space of time — speaking in geological terms — without leaving any fossil traces of the steps of the transformation. . . . As I have already implied, students of fossil primates have

not been distinguished for caution when working within the logical restraints of their subject. The record is so astonishing that it is legitimate to ask whether much science is yet to be found in this field at all."

64 *Weekend Australian*, magazine section, May 7–8, 1983, p.3.

65 *Nature*, Oxnard, vol. 258, 1975; also Charles E. Oxnard, *The Order of Man* (New Haven, CT: Yale University Press, 1984).

66 Richard E. Leakey, *The Making of Mankind* (London: Michael Joseph Limited, 1981), p. 43.

67 "Evolution," Encyclopedia Britannica Online, <http://members.eb.com/bol/topic?eu=108619&sctn=9>

68 See "Half-life" in the Merriam-Webster Dictionary.

69 See "Dating," Encyclopedia Britannica Online, <http://members.eb.com/bol/topic?eu=128006&sctn=2>; also *Physical Geology 7th Edition*, Plummer & McGeary, 1996.

70 The "isochron" technique for dealing with the chemical analyses of rocks being "dated" attempts to bypass this assumption. For a treatment of isochron "dating," along with the associated problems of false isochrons, see S.A. Austin, *Grand Canyon: Monument to Catastrophe* (El Cajon, CA: Institute for Creation Research, 1994), p. 111–131.

71 "Dating," Encyclopedia Britannica Online, <http://members.eb.com/bol/topic?eu=128006&sctn=2>, emphasis added. Such reasoning is deeper implied in the article in the Encyclopedia: "It is the obligation of geochronologists to try to prove themselves wrong by including a series of cross-checks in their measurements before they publish a result. Such checks include dating a series of ancient units with closely spaced but *known relative ages*. . . ." This means that in order to cross-check his or her radiometric dates, the geochronologist must rely on the geologist's already assumed age, or "known relative age," of the specimen to be dated. Such assumed ages, or "known relative ages," are derived from the geologic column — but see Woodmorappe, *Studies in Flood Geology*.

72 Radiometric "clocks" begin keeping time only after molten rock solidifies; i.e., radiometric dating should reveal the age of the rock from the time it hardened until the moment of dating.

73 *CEN Technical Journal*, 10(3), 1986.

74 This and many other examples published in scientific literature are documented in A.A. Snelling, *Proceedings of the Fourth International Conference on Creationism*, 1998, p.503–525. See also "Radioactive 'Dating' Failure," by Andrew Snelling, <http://www.answersingenesis.org/home/area/magazines/docs/cenv22n1_dating_failure.asp#f5>

75 J.G. Funkenhouser & John J. Naughton, "Radiogenic Helium and Argon in Ultramafic Inclusions from Hawaii," *Journal of Geophysical Research*, vol. 73, no.14, p. 4602.

76 Ian McDougall, H.A. Polach, J.J. Stipp, "Excess Radiogenic Argon in Young Subaerial Basalts from the Auckland Volcanic Field, New Zealand," *Geochimica et Cosmochimica Acta*, vol. 33, p. 1485.

77 A. Hayatsu (Department of Geophysics, University of Western Ontario, Canada), "K-Ar Isochron Age of the North Mountain Basalt, Nova Scotia," *Canadian Journal of Earth Sciences*, vol. 16, 1979, p. 974.

78 "Dating," Encyclopedia Britannica Online, <http://members.eb.com/bol/topic?eu=128006&sctn=1>

79 "Physics, Faith and the FBI," *Creation Ex Nihilo* magazine, December 2000–February 2001.

80 Sarfati, *Refuting Evolution*, p. 112.

81 Fredrick B. Jeaneman, "Secular Catastrophism," *Industrial Research and Development,* June 1982, p. 21.

82 Russell Humphreys, *Starlight and Time* (Green Forest, AR: Master Books, 1994).

83 This is in fact consistent with the Bible, which indicates 15 times, using three separate Hebrew verbs, that God "stretched," or "spread," out the heavens (Isa. 42:5, 45:12, 51:13; Jer. 10:12). In this biblical context, the word "heavens" is an ancient term for what is now called "space."

84 Humphreys uses the distortion of time in general relativity theory to explain how light could have reached the earth from distant stars in a much younger (by earth-bound clocks) universe. His theory also postulates a universe commencing not from some small point, but rather from a size only about 50 times more compact than today.

85 *Creation ex nihilo*, September–November 1999.

86 Some argue that the author of this biblical story was merely referring to a *localized* flood, and not worldwide. However, in itself, the biblical case for a *global* flood is strong. More than 30 statements of the universal character of the Flood and its effects occur in Genesis 6 through 9. God's purpose for sending the Flood was to destroy not only all mankind for their extreme wickedness, but also all animal life on the dry land as well (Gen. 6:7, 6:17, 7:22). The Flood lasted over a year (Gen. 7:11; 8:13), and many subsequent biblical writers accepted the historicity of the worldwide Flood (note Ps. 104:6–9; Isa. 54:9; 1 Pet. 3:20; 2 Pet. 2:5, 3:6; Heb. 11:7). It is these and many other biblical proofs which show that not only the author of the Book of Genesis but the other biblical authors as well accepted that the Flood was of worldwide extent and effect.

87 Many believe that the evidence and arguments from science stack up overwhelmingly against a literal interpretation of the Flood story. Where, for example, would such a volume of water have come from, and where would it have gone afterward? How would mammalian life have re-emerged on isolated islands and landmasses that emerged from the receding flood waters? Feasible scientific answers to such objections do in fact exist, yet the treatment that follows in this section regarding Noah's ark and the global Flood is brief. For a comprehensive treatment, consult the book by John Woodmorappe, *Noah's Ark: A Feasibility Study* (Santee, CA: Institute for Creation Research, 1996), a compilation of over seven years of study concerning issues such as food requirements, excretory requirements, pitch, interbreeding, animal migration after the Flood, and more. See also Don Batten, editor, *The Answers Book* (Green Forest, AR: Master Books, 1990), chapter 12, page 157, or look up "Flood" under the Q&A section of the Answers in Genesis website at <http://www.answersingenesis.org/home/area/faq/flood.asp>.

88 "Sedimentary rock," Encyclopedia Britannica Online, <http://members.eb.com/bol/topic?eu=117862&sctn=1>

89 In most cases, the Genesis "kind" could be equivalent to what is today called a *genus*, which is simply a broader grouping of animals than a species. Due to a process called rapid post-Flood speciation, many different species could have descended from one genus. That new species can be generated in a matter of years or decades has been observed. Both creationists and evolutionists have compiled numerous examples of such. Such speciation is the result of natural selection, that is, a sorting or removal of genetic information causing a loss of genetic diversity. For example, by selecting individual dogs which are very large or very small, Great Danes and Chihuahuas were bred. But these breeds have lost the information contained in their genes for certain other sizes; see the section "Mutations — Evolution's Raw Material" in this chapter. Also, animals such as tigers and lions can interbreed and produce hybrids called tigons and ligers, so it is likely that such animals descended from the same original kind.

90 Up-to-date tabulations as recorded in Woodmorappe's book, *Noah's Ark: A Feasibility Study*.

91 This type of survival has been observed, see *Nature*, October 8, 1998, p. 556.

92 The ark's measurements were 300x50x30 cubits (Gen. 6:15). One cubit is considered to be at least 18 inches in length.

93 Up-to-date tabulations as recorded in John Woodmorappe's book, *Noah's Ark: A Feasibility Study*, 1996. Note that many animals were probably adult-size by the time of disembarkment.

94 Creationists generally believe there was one great Ice Age after, and as a consequence of, the Flood. How a Genesis flood would have caused an Ice Age is explained in meteorologist Michael Oard's technical book, *An Ice Age Caused by the Genesis Flood* (El Cajon, CA: Institute for Creation Research, 1990). The Ice Age/Flood model offers a good explanation for issues such as frozen mammoths, land bridges, and more.

95 *New Scientist*, August 24, 1991.

96 When studying the development and origin of languages, there is strong evidence that supports this view. See *Creation ex nihilo*, vol. 22, no.1, 2000.

97 Alan Charig, *A New Look at the Dinosaurs* (New York, NY: Facts on file, Inc., 1983).

98 *Time*, November 30, 1998; also *Nature*, November 19, 1998.

99 Ibid.

100 "It is important to note that extinction is a normal, universal occurrence." ("Dinosaur," Encyclopedia Britannica Online, <http://members.eb.com/bol/topic?eu=108938&sctn=1>)

101 "Tyrannosaurus, Expeditions: Treasures," American Museum of Natural History, <http://www.amnh.org/exhibitions/expeditions/treasure_fossil/Treasures/Tyrannosaurus/tyrannos.html>

102 For instance, today's killer *piranhas* have relatives called the *pacus* who are plant-eaters, yet look virtually identical to the killer piranhas. Even experts found it hard to determine based on appearance whether a specimen was a piranha or pacu. See "Piranha," *Creation Ex Nihilo*, September–November 2000.

103 This is consistent within the creation model framework, which says that dinosaurs did not become extinct 65 million years ago, but were created by God at the same time as the other land animals. Most of the fossilized dinosaur bones found in the earth today would have been produced by the Genesis flood, along with many of the other fossils.

104 "Dragon," Encyclopedia Britannica Online, <http://members.eb.com/bol/topic?eu=31636&sctn=1>

105 "Lambeosaurus," Encyclopedia Britannica Online, <http://members.eb.com/bol/topic?eu=48028&sctn=1>

106 "Ground beetle," Encyclopedia Britannica Online, <http://members.eb.com/bol/topic?eu=38993&sctn=1>

107 "Life," Encyclopedia Britannica Online, <http://members.eb.com/ bol/topic?eu=109621&sctn=1>. Leading evolutionist Richard Dawkins also observes, "There is enough information capacity in a single human cell to store the *Encyclopedia Britannica,* all 30 volumes of it, three or four times over." Richard Dawkins, *The Blind Watchmaker* (New York, NY: Norton 1986), p. 115.

108 "Life," Encyclopedia Britannica Online, <http://members.eb.com/ bol/topic?eu=109621&sctn=1>

109 Michael Denton, *Evolution: A Theory in Crisis* (Bethesda, MD: Adler & Adler, 1986).

110 Ibid.

111 Fred Hoyle, *The Intelligent Universe* (New York, NY: Holt, Rinehart, and Winston, 1983). This figure has been criticized by some because it assumes present complex enzymes and production of all 2,000 enzymes at once, however, the necessity of a large number of enzymes to sustain life is unquestioned by scientists.

112 "Sir Fred Hoyle," Encyclopedia Britannica Online, <http:// members.eb.com/bol/topic?eu=42169&sctn=1>

113 Hoyle, *The Intelligent Universe.*

114 Ibid.

115 Francis Crick & L.E. Orgel, "Directed Panspermia," *Icarus* journal, 19, p. 341–346; also Francis Crick, *Life Itself* (New York, NY: Simon and Schuster, 1981).

116 "Francis Crick," Encyclopedia Britannica Online, <http:// members.eb.com/bol/topic?eu=28338&sctn=1>

117 The complex, meaningful arrangement of bases (or "letters") in the DNA code are characterized by high specified complexity, that is, high information content. Leading origin-of-life researcher Leslie Orgel, explains: "Living things are distinguished by their specified complexity. . . . Roughly speaking, the information content of a structure is the minimum number of instructions needed to specify the structure." The more complex a structure is, the more instructions needed to specify it. Leslie Orgel, *The Origins of Life* (New York, NY: Wiley, 1973), p.189–190. For a more detailed explanation of how information theory relates to biology, see "DNA, Design, and the Origin of Life," <http:// www.origins.org/offices/thaxton/docs/thaxton_dna.html>.

118 "There is no known natural law through which matter can give rise to information, neither is any physical process or material phenomenon known that can do this." Werner Gitt, *In the Beginning Was Information*, 2nd English Edition (Bielefeld, Germany: CLV [Christliche Literatur-Verbreitung], 2000), p. 79. A distinction must

be made between *order* and *information*. A neat pattern of ice crystals, for example, does not contain meaningful information (specified complexity), it simply shows a repeated meaningless pattern of the same structure over and over. Also, examples such as Richard Dawkins' English sentence computer simulation, called "Methinks It Is Like a Weasel," attempt to downplay the information observed in living things. However, Dawkins' computer program will always reach its goal, because the whole design involves selecting a target in advance. The program is fixed, the target is specified in advance, and, ironically, all the parameters are set by an intelligent agent!

119 Neither a random nor a repetitive sequence would be proof, because natural processes produce radio noise from outer space, while pulsars produce regular signals.

120 There is much more information available. See <http://www.answersingenesis.org>

———◦◦———

CHAPTER FOUR

THE BIBLE AS PRE-SCIENTIFIC

*DOES THE BIBLE
SUPPORT OR
CONTRADICT
SCIENCE?*

No educated person today would hesitate to categorize the Bible as pre-scientific; obviously its ancient writings pre-date modern science by thousands of years.

Nonetheless, some biblical statements seem to reveal a relatively advanced knowledge of scientific matters. Unfortunately, however, these statements are sometimes taken out of context and misunderstood, and the Bible is thus thought to contain scientifically flawed information.

For example, in the 17th century, Galileo, a creationist,

proved that the earth revolves around the sun. However, the Catholic Church had accepted the majority view of the scientific establishment of the time, which said that the sun revolves around the earth. The church picked out a few verses (or statements) from the Bible which it thought supported this belief. These verses, however, were taken out of context.

For instance, in Psalm 93:1, the phrase "the [earth] is firmly established, it cannot be moved" needs to be read in context with the next verse, "[God's] throne was established long ago," where the same Hebrew word [*kown* = "established"] is used and has the meaning "set up," "stable," "secure," "enduring," etc., and *not* "immobile" or "stationary." Likewise, the Hebrew word for "moved" (in Ps. 93:1) is also used in Psalm 16:8, "I will not be moved," meaning that the writer of that verse would not stray from the path of God, not that he was physically rooted to any one geographic spot. Understood correctly then, Psalm 93:1 implies that the earth itself also moves along a path from which it cannot stray.

It can thus be seen that only the 17th century Catholic Church's understanding of this biblical statement was incorrect, and not the statement itself. Ironically, had the church not accepted the incorrect majority view of the then scientific establishment, the Bible may have been seen to be correct all along, and the false ensuing notion that the Bible contradicts science may possibly have been avoided.[1]

It is often little realized that the Bible does, in fact, seem to contain remarkably accurate scientific information. This chapter presents several examples.[2]

ANCIENT MEDICAL PRACTICES

To gain an understanding of the primitive level of medical and sanitary knowledge possessed by the ancient Egyptians of the Mid-East region about 3,500 years ago, the *Ebers Papyrus* is valuable and important. One of the oldest known medical works, this compilation of medical texts dates to about 1550 B.C.[3]

Despite their advanced knowledge of astronomy and engineering, as evidenced by the world-famous pyramids, much of the Egyptians' medical understanding was extremely primitive and sometimes even dangerous.[4] Consider, for example, the Egyptian doctor's suggestion for healing an infected splinter wound, involving the application of an ointment mixture composed of the blood of worms mixed with the dung of a donkey. Other prescriptions included lizards' blood, swines' teeth, putrid meat, stinking fat, moisture from pigs' ears, milk, goose grease, asses' hooves, animal fats from various sources, excreta from animals, including humans, donkeys, antelopes, dogs, cats, and even flies.[5]

In contrast to such hazardous practices, the Bible's instructions on certain medical procedures and basic sanitation rules during the same time period prove much more advanced. For example, with regard to the use of things like cooking tools, the Old Testament gives detailed orders that would have prevented the spread of germs from animal carcasses.[6] This is surprising because, until the 19th century, even medical researchers and doctors did not know that disease could be transmitted by microscopic germs or viruses.[7] Another passage in the Bible instructs that "the fat of a beast that dies naturally and the fat of what is torn by wild animals, may be used in any other way; but you shall by no means eat it" (Lev. 7:24). It is now known that any animal carcass found after natural death would be dangerous to eat because it would likely contain the infectious germs that would develop within hours of an animal's death.

The biblical Book of Numbers specifies incredible instructions on cleansing and purifying someone who had become defiled due to touching a dead body (Num. 19). The water of purification described in this biblical narrative actually had the ability to destroy germs and infection. This water of purification solution contained ashes from a red heifer sacrifice combined with cedar, hyssop, and scarlet. The "cedar" oil came from a kind of juniper tree that grew in both Israel and in the Sinai. Cedar wood is an astringent for oily and congested skin conditions, acne, and dandruff. It relieves dermatitis, insect bites, and itching. Cedar oil contains thujene, which eliminates warts, and irritates the skin,[8] encouraging the person to vigorously rub the solution into his or her hands. More importantly, the hyssop plant used in the solution would produce hyssop oil.[9] This oil is actually a very effective antiseptic and antibacterial agent, containing carvacrol, which is still used as a fungicide and disinfectant today.[10]

One of the more notable medical details in the Bible is found in the specific instructions regarding the process of circumcising every Hebrew male child at the age of eight days old (Gen. 17:12). Interestingly, the two specific factors necessary to facilitate blood clotting and thus prevent fatal hemorrhaging, vitamin K and prothrombin, are at their highest levels (110 percent of normal) on the eighth day of life. Scientists have discovered that vitamin K is formed in the blood of a baby between day five to day seven of the baby's life. Thus, of all the days of a baby's life, the eighth day is the optimum day for an operation.[11]

The *Encyclopedia Britannica's* conclusion regarding the Bible's instructions on sanitary and medical practices is fitting: "The Old Testament is a mine of information on social and personal hygiene. The Jews were indeed pioneers in matters of public health."[12]

ADVANCED SCIENCE

Ignorant of today's scientific knowledge, the ancient biblical writers dared to make several bold statements about the universe. For instance, in certain passages the ancients wrote about water, and even ice, in space (Gen. 1:6–7; Job 38:29).

Today, each large comet is calculated to contain as much as one trillion tons of ice.[13]

Another biblical statement may reveal some knowledge of the effect of gravity on the earth thousands of years before Isaac Newton proved it: "[God] hangs the earth on nothing" (Job 26:7). Up until the last few centuries, scientists believed that the earth and stars were supported by some kind of medium. Of course, the earth actually just "hangs" or orbits in space.

The ancient writers even commented about the earth's weather patterns: "[God] draws up the water vapor and then distils it into rain. The rain pours down from the clouds" (Job 36:27–29). Though simply stated, this biblical passage, written thousands of years ago, reveals the complete hydrological cycle of evaporation, cloud formation, and precipitation. Not until recently have these hydrological cycles been scientifically determined.

Many are familiar with the creation of man story as told in the biblical Book of Genesis: "And the Lord God formed man of the dust of the ground, and breathed into his nostrils the breath of life; and man became a living being" (Gen. 2:7). For years many have laughed at the apparent simplicity of the biblical idea that God used "the dust of the ground" to construct the complex elements and molecules that make up a human being. But a late discovery made by researchers at NASA's AMES Research Center proved that every single element found in the human body exists within the earth of the ground. The scientists concluded, "We are just beginning to learn. The biblical scenario for the creation of life turns out to be not far off the mark."[14]

Footnotes

1 "The Galileo 'Twist,' " *Creation Ex Nihilo* magazine, September–November 1997. Galileo's conflict with the Roman Catholic Church was not between science and religion, as usually portrayed. Rather it

was a conflict between Copernican science (earth revolves around the sun) and Aristotelian science (sun revolves around the earth — this incorrect view was supported by the church).

2 Many of the examples as listed here are derived from *The Signature of God* by Grant Jeffrey (Nashville, TN: Word, 1996).

3 "Ebers Papyrus," Encyclopedia Britannica Online, <http://members.eb.com/bol/topic?eu=32397&sctn=1>

4 However, some of their knowledge of the human body was surprisingly accurate, such as their description of the circulatory system.

5 From the Ebers Papyrus manuscript, as translated in *A Sketch of Medicine and Pharmacy*, S.E. Massengill (Bristol, TN: The S.E. Massengill Co., 1940).

6 The biblical passage reads: "Any object on which the dead body of an animal falls will be defiled [forbidden to be used or touched]. If it is a clay oven or cooking pot, it must be smashed to pieces. It has become defiled, and it will remain that way" (Lev. 11:35).

7 "Semmelweis Ignaz Philipp," Encyclopedia Britannica Online, <http://members.eb.com/bol/topic?eu=68445&sctn=1>

8 Kathy Keville and Mindy Green, *Aromatherapy: A Complete Guide to the Healing Art* (Freedom, CA: Crossing Press, 1995).

9 This plant in Hebrew is called *ezov*, probably a species of "savory" according to Encyclopedia Britannica (Hyssop).

10 "Savory," Encyclopedia Britannica Online; also "Carvacrol," Merriam-Webster Dictionary; also *None of These Diseases*, S.I. McMillen, (Old Tappan, NJ: F.H. Revell Co., 1984).

11 According to an interview with Dr. Nelles Silverthorne on *100 Huntley Street*. Dr. Silverthorne's contributions to managing infectious diseases are well documented in the annals of The Hospital for Sick Children in Toronto. Silverthorne is a medical researcher who, according to the interview, put up the world's first oxygen tent at that hospital, gave the world's first civilian injection of penicillin, and developed a treatment that is used today for meningitis.

12 "History of Medicine," Encyclopedia Britannica Online, <http://members.eb.com/bol/topic?eu=119072&sctn=2>

13 On June 30, 1908, a block of ice from space weighing 30,000 tons collided with the earth in Siberia, releasing energy equivalent to that of a thermonuclear bomb of 12 megatons. J. Audouze, *The Cambridge Atlas of Astronomy* (New York, NY: Cambridge University Press, 1985).

14 *Reader's Digest*, November 1982

———◆———

Chapter Five

WHAT
IS A
CONTRADICTION?

ARE THERE
CONTRADICTIONS
WITHIN THE BIBLE?

Skeptics often pose the question "How can one believe a Bible that is full of contradictions?" The question assumes that the Bible is filled with so many obvious discrepancies, it would be foolish to trust it.

However, while certain passages, at first glance, may appear contradictory (as can the testimonies of any two honest witnesses in one legal trial), further investigation may show otherwise.

What constitutes a contradiction? The law of contradiction, which is the basis of all logical thinking, states that a thing cannot be both *a* and *non-a* at the same time, in the same place, and in the same manner.[1] It cannot be both raining and not raining at the same time in the same location. If one can demonstrate a violation of this principle in the Bible, then one can prove a contradiction. For example, if the Bible said that Jesus died by crucifixion both at Jerusalem and at Nazareth at the same time, this would be a provable error.

When looking at possible contradictions, it is important to note that two statements can differ from each other without being contradictory. It can be easy to confuse *contradiction* with *difference*. For example:

Suppose you talk to the mayor of your city and the chief of police at city hall. Later, you see your friend, Jim, and tell him you talked to the mayor today. An hour after that, you see another friend, John, and tell him you talked to both the mayor and the chief of police. Your friends compare notes, and there seems to be a contradiction — but there is not. Since you had not told Jim you talked *only* to the mayor, you did not contradict what you told John.[2]

The statements made to Jim and John were *different*, but not contradictory. Neither statement denies the other; rather, they are complementary. Many biblical statements fall into this category, and people sometimes think they find errors in passages when actually, they simply do not read the passages correctly.

When two passages are taken out of context, alleged contradictions can be found in almost any document, including, for example, the *Encyclopedia Britannica*. In one article, which discusses the persecution of Christians, the encyclopedia reads:

Persecution of Christians *first* arose in connection with converts among the Greek-speaking Jews in Jerusalem.[3] (This event occurred sometime between A.D. 30–35.)

Yet, another article regarding Christian persecution in the same encyclopedia reads:

> The *first* persecution, that of Nero, was related to a devastating fire in the capital in A.D. *64*.[4]

On the surface, this seems to be a direct contradiction: How can the first persecution of Christians be both before A.D. 35 and in A.D. 64? However, when each passage is studied within its original context, the intended meaning becomes clear, and the contradiction disappears. In reality, A.D. 30–35 is when the *Jews* first began persecuting Christians, and A.D. 64 is when the *Roman authorities* first officially persecuted them.

For the most part, the contradictions presented by many Bible critics tend to be nothing more than innocent misunderstandings, manipulations of archaic words, or a failure to give the text a fair chance to prove itself. To clarify such alleged contradictions, all relevant facts must be considered (if possible), and then a conclusion should be drawn providing the simplest possible explanation.

Here are possible solutions to some frequently published alleged biblical contradictions:[5]

> Genesis 1 (God creates plants, then animals,
>   then man and woman)
> Genesis 2 (God creates man, then plants, then
>   animals, then woman)

After chronologically tracing the creation of the universe in chapter 1, the theme narrows in chapter 2 to focus on man's place in the universe. Genesis 1 is meant to be a step-by-step historical account, while Genesis 2 is more of a summary. Reading the two passages should easily convince anyone of this. Genesis 2 is not concerned so much with time frames, but events. If one carefully reads the events in Genesis 2 (in the NIV), one would see that as man is mentioned, it is noted that the Garden had already been created. When animals are brought into the picture, this is similarly noted.[6]

> Matthew 27:5 (Judas hangs himself)
> Acts 1:18 (Judas falls headlong, his bowels gush)

How did Judas die? The Book of Matthew says he hung himself. The Book of Acts says he fell down and burst. A logical explanation is that after Judas hung himself and was eventually cut down, his body fell headlong and burst open. Why would his body have "burst open" falling down in a field unless it was in some state of decomposition?

> Acts 1:18 (Judas purchased the field with the 30 pieces of silver)
> Matthew 27:6–7 (The chief priests purchased the field with the 30 pieces of silver)

The account states that Judas received a reward of 30 pieces of silver for betraying Jesus, but afterward tried to return it to the chief priests who gave it to him. When they refused, Judas threw down the money and went to hang himself. The chief priests then picked up the money, according to the account, and decided to buy a potter's field with it. Since Judas' reward money was used to purchase the field where he was buried, he was thus ultimately the real buyer of the field. Acts 1 is a quick summary of the events after the resurrection of Jesus, and the statements made are not out of line with the style of writing.

> Luke 17:34 (Jesus' final return "in the last days" will be during the nighttime)

Luke 17:30–31 (Jesus' final return "in the last
days" will be during the daytime)

To the natural mind of Luke's time, these words of Jesus
must have sounded like a contradiction. People would have
thought, *How could a single event occur simultaneously in the
day and in the night?* Such a statement must have appeared
just as impossible and contradictory in the first century as it
does now. Of course, it is now understood that it could be a
daytime event for those on one side of the globe, while the
event could occur simultaneously in the night for those living
on the other side of the planet.

———※———

Any attorney who has faced the task of piecing together
apparently conflicting courtroom testimony can understand
how difficult it is to reconcile an apparent contradiction between two witnesses. The Cambridge-educated Sir Norman
Anderson, who lectured at Princeton University, was offered
a professorship for life at Harvard University, and served as
dean of the Faculty of Law at the University of London,[7] states:

> I must confess that I am appalled by the way in
> which some people — biblical scholars among them
> — are prepared to make the most categorical state-
> ments that this story cannot possibly be reconciled
> with that, or that such and such statements are
> wholly irreconcilable, when a little gentle question-
> ing of the witnesses, were this possible, might well
> have cleared up the whole problem. Sometimes,
> indeed, a tentative solution may not be very far to
> seek even without such questioning, although the
> suggested reconciliation cannot, of course, be
> proved; and in others there may well be a perfectly
> satisfactory solution which evades us.[8]

Concerning the New Testament Gospels in particular, Lee Strobel, former award-winning legal editor of the *Chicago Tribune*, points out, "Ironically, if the gospels had been identical to each other, word for word, this would have raised charges that the authors had conspired among themselves to coordinate their stories in advance, and that would have cast doubt on them." Craig Blomberg, who is widely considered to be one of the foremost authorities on the biographies of Jesus, affirms, "If the gospels were too consistent, that in itself would invalidate them as independent witnesses."[9]

A classical historian, German scholar Hans Stier, says that agreement over basic data and *divergence* of details suggest credibility, because fabricated accounts tend to be fully consistent and harmonized. "Every historian," he wrote, "is especially skeptical at that moment when an extraordinary happening is only reported in accounts which are completely free of contradictions."[10]

In fact, sometimes the solutions to biblical differences reveal just how precisely the writers have communicated the events that have occurred; such differences can actually become confirmations of the Bible's minute accuracy and trustworthiness.

Footnotes

1 See "Laws of thought," Encyclopedia Britannica Online, <http://members.eb.com/bol/topic?eu=74149&sctn=1>.

2 This example, and other parts of this chapter, is from *Evidence That Demands a Verdict*, by Josh McDowell (Nashville, TN: T. Nelson, 1993).

3 "Paul the Apostle," Encyclopedia Britannica Online, <http://members.eb.com/bol/topic?artcl=108605&seq_nbr=1&page=n&isctn=2>. Emphasis added.

4 "Ancient Rome," Encyclopedia Britannica Online, <http://members.eb.com/bol/topic?eu=109199&sctn=6>. Emphasis added.

5 The explanations given may or may not be correct; what is important is that the solutions only show a plausible explanation. If a logical explanation can be found, then the critic's assertion that "x and y are contradictory" becomes negligible.

6 Between the creation of Adam and the creation of Eve in Genesis chapter 2, the KJV Bible says "Out of the ground the Lord God formed every beast of the field, and every fowl of the air" (Gen. 2:19). On the surface, this seems to say that the land creatures and birds were created between the creation of Adam and Eve. However, ancient Hebrew scholars apparently did not recognize any conflict with the account in chapter 1, where Adam and Eve were both created after the creatures and birds (Gen. 1:23–25). Why is this? Because in Hebrew the precise tense of a verb is determined by the context. It is clear from chapter 1 that the beasts and birds were created before Adam, so Hebrew scholars would have understood the verb "formed" in Genesis 2:19 to mean "had formed" or "having formed." If verse 19 is translated as follows (as in the NIV), "Now the LORD God had formed out of the ground all the beasts of the field," the apparent disagreement with Genesis 1 disappears completely. Many people wrongly assume that Genesis 2 is just a different account of creation to that in Genesis 1. However, it should be evident that Genesis 2 is not meant as another account of creation because it says nothing about the creation of the heavens and the earth, the atmosphere, the seas, the land, the sun, the stars, the moon, the sea creatures, etc. Genesis 2 mentions only things directly relevant to the creation of Adam and Eve and their life in the Garden that God prepared specially for them. Genesis 1 may be understood as creation from God's perspective; it is "the big picture," an overview of the whole. Genesis 2 views the more important aspects from man's perspective. (This footnote is largely derived from the article "Genesis Contradictions?" by Don Batten, Answers in Genesis, <http://www.answersingenesis.org/docs/1272.asp>.)

7 Lee Strobel, *The Case for Christ* (Grand Rapids, MI: Zondervan, 1998).

8 Sir Norman Anderson, *Jesus Christ: The Witness of History* (Downers Grove, IL: Inter-Varsity Press, 1985), p.139.

9 All the quotes in this paragraph are from *The Case for Christ* by Lee Strobel.

10 Ibid.

CHAPTER SIX

UNPARALLELED HISTORICITY

IS THE TEXT OF THE BIBLE A RELIABLE HISTORICAL DOCUMENT?

I t is often believed that the text of today's Bible could not possibly be authentic — many of the words and sentences must have been tampered with, or altered over time. After all, the events described date back thousands of years — plenty of time for error to creep in. Indeed, if the children's game of "broken telephone" teaches anything, it is surely that the original story will become corrupted after being passed from one person to the next. Especially would this be the case if many generations of people were involved.

Amazingly, this has not been the case for the Bible's Old Testament. In 1947, young Arab shepherds, searching for a stray goat in the Judean Desert, entered a long-untouched cave in the ruins of Qumran and accidentally fumbled across several jars filled with ancient biblical scrolls. This discovery yielded seven scrolls and began a search that lasted nearly a decade, eventually producing thousands of scroll fragments from 11 caves. Historical, paleographic, and linguistic evidence, as well as carbon-14 dating, established that the scrolls dated from approximately 3 B.C. to A.D. 68.[1] Originating at the time when Jesus lived, they are older than any other surviving biblical manuscripts by almost one thousand years. These scrolls were first displayed in the United States at the Library of Congress in 1949, but are housed today in the Shrine of the Book in Jerusalem.[2]

Along with several other writings, all 39 books of the Bible's Old Testament were represented in the Dead Sea Scroll collection (with the exception of the Book of Esther). With few negligible variations, these ancient scrolls proved to be "practically identical" in content to today's version of the Old Testament,[3] demonstrating that even over a 2,000-year period, the biblical text has managed to remain free from corruption.

SHAKING MODERN DISCOVERIES

While it is generally agreed that the text of the Bible has remained free from corruption, liberal scholars still criticize the Bible concerning its historical reliability. Such criticisms have usually been based on a lack of archaeological evidence to confirm the biblical record.

Today, however, the credibility of such criticisms is steadily diminishing. Canada's *National Post* illuminates, "Archaeologists are increasingly discovering that their finds support the Bible's account of many historical events, from Roman crucifixion practices to ancient battles and the existence of King David. . . . The Bible has even provided archaeologists with leads to discoveries they may never have otherwise uncovered. More and more, archaeological finds are affirming the historical accuracy of the Bible, corroborating key portions of events."[4]

Following are several such discoveries, some of which have stunned liberal scholars.

According to the biblical account, King David was the founder of Israel's city of Jerusalem — 1996 was celebrated as Jerusalem's 3,000th anniversary as the "City of David." The biblical story of King David is so fantastic that scholars have claimed for decades that the existence of David and his conquests were pure fiction. However, in 1993 archaeologists unearthed a piece of stone from an ancient monument. Inscribed on it in ancient Aramaic were the words "King of Israel" and "House of David." Initially unbelievable, this discovery has since been described as "one of the greatest finds of the 20th century" by the director of one of the world's leading archaeological institutes. The Associated Press conveys, "The discovery so shook some scholars that they insisted the find was phony or the inscription incorrectly translated. A year later, however, archaeologists found more fragments of the monument with additional inscriptions referring to the ancient king. Today, the new scholarly consensus is that David was real — because archaeology has found it."[5]

The *U.S. News & World Report* explains why this "reference to David was a historical bombshell: never before had the familiar name of Judah's ancient warrior king, a central figure of the Hebrew Bible and, according to Christian Scripture, an ancestor of Jesus, been found in the records of antiquity outside the pages of the Bible. Skeptics had long seized upon that fact to argue that David was a mere legend, invented by Hebrew scribes. Now, at last, there was material evidence: an inscription written not by Hebrew scribes but by an enemy of the Israelites a little more than a century after David's presumptive lifetime."[6]

Following are some additional finds of importance:[7]

- Recent expeditions at Shechem, where the Bible says Abraham built an altar to God, prove an organized community existed there during Abraham's time nearly 4,000 years ago.

- Archaeologists have found a stone tablet with an inscription bearing the name of the city of Ekron, which is the city where, according to the Book of First Samuel in the Bible, the Philistines took the ark of the covenant after capturing it from the Israelites.

- Recent excavations have uncovered a string of ancient Egyptian forts along the Mediterranean coast. The discovery offers an explanation for why Moses would lead his people out of Egypt through the Sinai wilderness instead of along the shorter coastal route, as the story in Exodus relates.

- During the summer of 1996, a wine jug was found inscribed with the name of King Herod, the first object ever found bearing the Judean king's name from the New Testament Gospels.

- An ivory pomegranate [a tropical reddish fruit] purchased in the international antiquities market by Israeli authorities for $550,000 in 1988 is now believed by many scholars to be the first relic ever found from Solomon's Temple. According to the Bible, the magnificent temple — generally dated to around 950 B.C. – housed the ark of the covenant. An inscription on the pomegranate has been translated as "Holy to the priests, belonging to the temple of Yahweh [the LORD]."

Additional discoveries that proved amazingly consistent with the biblical narratives of Jesus Christ were reported in a 1999 cover article in *U.S. News & World Report*:

Compared with the earlier eras of Old Testament history, the days of Jesus are a fleeting moment. A life span of just three decades and a public career of only a few years leave a dauntingly narrow target for archaeological exploration. Yet during the past four decades, spectacular discoveries have produced a wealth of data illuminating the story of Jesus and the birth of Christianity. The picture that has emerged overall closely matches the historical back-drop of the Gospels.

In 1968, for example, explorers found the skel-etal remains of a crucified man in a burial cave out-side of Jerusalem. It was a momentous discovery: While the Romans were known to have crucified thousands of alleged traitors, rebels, robbers, and deserters, never before had the remains of a cruci-fixion victim been recovered. An initial analysis of the remains found that their condition dramatically corroborated the Bible's description of the Roman method of execution.

The bones were preserved in a stone burial box and appeared to be those of a man about 5 feet, 5 inches tall. His open arms had been nailed to the crossbar, in the manner similar to that shown in crucifixion paintings. The knees had been doubled up and turned sideways, and a single large iron nail had been driven through both heels. The shin bones seem to have been broken, corroborating what the Gospel of John suggests was normal practice in Roman crucifixions: "Then the soldiers came and broke the legs of the first and of the other who had been crucified with him. But when they came to Jesus and saw that he was already dead, they did not break his legs" (John 19:32–33).

The discovery posed a powerful counter-argument to objections some scholars have raised against the Gospels' description of Jesus' burial. It has been argued that the common practice of Roman executioners was to toss corpses of crucified criminals into a common grave or to leave them on the cross to be devoured by scavenging animals. So it hardly seems feasible that Roman authorities would have allowed Jesus to undergo the burial described in the Gospels. But with the remains of a crucified contemporary of Jesus found in a family grave, it is clear that at least on some occasions the Romans permitted proper interment consistent with the biblical account.

A few decades ago, the name of a key figure in the arrest and crucifixion of Jesus turned up in the archaeological record: During excavations in 1961 a first-century inscription was uncovered confirming that Pilate had been the Roman ruler of the region at the time of Jesus' crucifixion. The badly damaged Latin inscription reads in part, "[Pon]tius Pilatus . . . [Praef]ectus Juda[ea]e." According to experts, the inscription would have read, "Pontius Pilate, the Prefect of Judea." The discovery of the so-called Pilate Stone has been widely acclaimed as a significant affirmation of biblical history because, in short, it confirms that the man depicted in the Gospels as Judea's Roman governor had precisely the responsibilities and authority that the Gospel writers ascribed to him.

Thanks to archaeology, the Bible has been firmly fixed in a context of knowable history, linked to the present by footprints across the archaeological record.[8]

Today, the words of the great American archaeologist William Albright continue to ring profoundly true: "The excessive skepticism shown toward the Bible [by certain schools of thought] has been progressively discredited. Discovery after discovery has established the accuracy of numerous details."[9]

NON-BIBLICAL SOURCES

In relatively recent times, some have tried to dispute the fact that the Christian figure of Jesus Christ was an actual historical person. Jesus, they say, never really lived, but was fabricated in the imaginations of those who founded Christianity.

However, there are several surviving *non*-Christian documents from the 1st and 2nd centuries A.D. which confirm not only the historicity of Jesus, but also the following information about Him: 1) Jesus was a Jewish teacher; 2) many people believed that He performed healings and exorcisms; 3) He was rejected by the Jewish leaders; 4) He was crucified under Pontius Pilate in the reign of Tiberius (A.D. 14–37); 5) despite this shameful death, his followers, who believed that He was still alive, spread beyond Palestine so that there were multitudes of them in Rome by A.D. 64; 6) all kinds of people from the cities and countryside — men and women, slave and free — worshiped Him as God by the beginning of the 2nd century.[10]

As the *Encyclopedia Britannica* observes, the non-Christian accounts that corroborate the above facts "prove that in ancient times even the opponents of Christianity never doubted the historicity of Jesus, which was disputed for the first time and on inadequate grounds at the end of the 18th, during the 19th, and at the beginning of the 20th centuries."[11]

The Encyclopedia lists the following historical accounts as examples:

1. *Antiquities of the Jews, by Flavius Josephus (A.D. 37–100).* This work is described as "invaluable" for Jewish history.[12] As a historian, with access to both Roman and Jewish governmental records, Josephus described events in Israel during the 1st century A.D. His work includes several references to Jesus Christ, one of which reads: "Now there was about this time Jesus, a wise man, if it be lawful to call him a man; for he was a doer of wonderful works, a teacher of such men as receive the truth with pleasure. He drew over to him both many of the Jews and many of the Gentiles. He was the Christ. And when Pilate, at the suggestion of the principal men amongst us, had condemned him to the cross, those that loved him at the first did not forsake him; for he appeared to them alive again the third day; as the divine prophets had foretold these and ten thousand other wonderful things concerning him. And the tribe of Christians, so named from him, are not extinct at this day."[13]

2. *The Annals* [historical records] *of the Roman historian and governor of Asia, Cornelius Tacitus, written about A.D. 110.* These writings confirm such things as the execution of Jesus, identify Jesus as the founder of the Christian faith, and discuss the persecution of Christians.[14]

3. *An inquiry of the governor of Asia Minor, Plinius Secundus (Pliny the Younger), in his letter to the emperor Trajan (A.D. 111).* Here, Christians are described as those who "bound themselves to a solemn oath" and sang hymns to Christ "as to a god."[15]

4. *Roman historian, Suetonius, in his Life of Claudius (A.D. 100).* Suetonius refers to the Christians causing disturbances in

Rome which led to their being banished from the city.[16] Claudius's decree of expulsion (A.D. 49) is also mentioned in the Bible (Acts 18:2).

5. *The Talmud, a compendium of Jewish law, lore, and commentary.* (Referring to specific writings from the 1st and 2nd centuries). These writings reveal an acquaintance with the Christian tradition, but include several divergent legendary motifs as well. The picture of Jesus offered in these writings may be summarized as follows: born the (according to some interpretations, illegitimate) son of a man called Panther, Jesus worked magic, ridiculed the wise, seduced and stirred up the people, gathered five disciples about him, and was hanged (crucified) on the eve of the Passover.[17]

A BRIEF HISTORY OF THE NEW TESTAMENT

Probably the most famous group of New Testament skeptics is the "Jesus Seminar," a loosely connected group of scholars that meet twice a year to vote on the accuracy of the words and deeds of Jesus as written in the New Testament. Religious followers, they argue, composed the Gospels (the biographies of Jesus) many years after Jesus lived, and, for the most part, the accounts cannot be trusted as authentic.

This group, however, is out of sync even with the majority of liberal New Testament scholarship. The one historical fact that all scholars agree on — that Jesus was crucified — is impossible to explain after the Jesus Seminar excises 80 percent of His teachings from the New Testament. The Jesus Seminar ends up with a Jew who is stripped of his Jewishness, and the founder of a Church whose followers rarely bothered to actually quote him. Their portrayal of Jesus fails to account for the strong reactions of His contemporaries. The few words they judge authentic to Jesus reduce Him to an insipid eccentric who would have been powerless to create the strong reactions against Him that resulted in His crucifixion. As leading Catholic scholar John Meier puts it in his recent work on the historical Jesus, "A tweedy poetaster who spent his time spinning out parables and Japanese koans, a literary aesthete who toyed with first-century deconstructionism, or a bland Jesus who simply told people to look at the lilies of the field — such a Jesus would threaten no one, just as the university professors who create him threaten no one."[18]

In any case, most liberal scholars themselves also tend to be somewhat skeptical when studying the biographies of Jesus. They believe that the burden of proof rests not on themselves, but on any scholar who would claim authenticity for a particular saying of Jesus. This is contrary to the usual approach when examining ancient historians, however. Usually, if ancient writers prove trustworthy in cases where they can be tested, they are given the benefit of the doubt in cases where they cannot be tested. For instance, if an archaeological discovery verifies that at least some parts of an ancient document are historically reliable, it would normally be assumed that the remainder of the document is also reliable. Since the Gospel writers have repeatedly proved themselves in this respect, such reasoning should accordingly place the burden of proof on the skeptic who would claim otherwise.

When examining the historical reliability of the New Testament, certain standards of critique should be used that would normally apply to any document of the ancient world. What is important in such an analysis is how the New Testament compares to other works of the ancient world whose historicity is seldom called into question.

The following table displays five categories of several ancient writings:[19] 1) the author/writing; 2) the time period in which the writings are known to have been written; 3) the oldest copy in possession today; 4) the time gap between the original manuscript and the oldest copy in possession; and 5) the number of manuscript copies (fragments or otherwise) in existence today.

Author	When Written	Oldest Copy (±)	Time Gap	No. of Copies (±)
Caesar	100–44 B.C.	A.D. 900	1,000 years	10
Tacitus (Annals)	A.D. 100	A.D. 1,100	1,000 years	20
Pliny (History)	A.D. 61–113	A.D. 850	750 years	7
Plato (Tetralogies)	427–347 B.C.	A.D. 900	1,200 years	7
Aristotle	384–322 B.C.	A.D. 1,100	1,400 years	5
New Testament	A.D. 40–100	A.D. 130	30 years	24,000

It can be seen that, as far as the time gap between the original authorship of the New Testament and the earliest manuscripts in possession today, there is no work from the ancient world that can compare to the New Testament. But not only does a comparison of the time gap show that the New Testament is unparalleled in the ancient world, a comparison of the number of manuscripts in possession today shows the superiority of the New Testament as well. The *Encyclopedia Britannica* concedes, "Compared with other ancient manuscripts, the text of the New Testament is dependable and consistent."[20]

The significance of having a small time gap is that the closer a manuscript copy is to the original, the more accurate it is regarded as being, because there has been less time for mistakes to creep in during transmission.

Moreover, the significance of having a larger number of manuscripts is that the greater the number of manuscripts, the more certain the reading of the original can be.

To illustrate, suppose someone gave you a copy of a telegram written to you which said, "You have won one million #ollars!" As you read the copy you feel quite certain that what you have won is one million dollars, and that the number sign was merely a copyist's error. However, suppose that you received another copy of the telegram which read "You have won one &illion dollars!" With this additional copy you are more certain of your conclusion about the original telegram, since the "d" is present in the second copy where it was missing from the first, and the "m" is present in the first where it is missing from the second.

It is in this manner that literary scholars ascertain the reading of the original writing of an ancient document. Obviously, the more manuscripts in existence to cross-reference, the more reliable the reading of the original can be.

As Sir Frederic Kenyon, former director of the British Museum, has said, "The net result . . . is, in fact, to reduce the gap between the earlier manuscripts and the traditional dates of the New Testament books so far that it becomes negligible in any discussion of their authenticity. No other ancient book has anything like such an early and plentiful testimony to its text. . . . No unbiased scholar would deny that the text that has come down to us is substantially sound."[21] Furthermore, he says, "The general result of all these discoveries and all this study is to strengthen the proof of the authenticity of the Scriptures."[22] It can thus be firmly concluded, in Sir Frederick Kenyon's words, that "in substance the text of the Bible is certain: especially is this the case with the New Testament."[23]

In the end, when it comes to checking and cross-checking the readings of the New Testament, it stands as the most historically attested work of the ancient world. If a person discards the Bible as unreliable in this sense, then he or she must discard almost all the literature of the ancient world.

When Were the Gospels Written?

Most scholars place the autographs of the Gospels sometime before A.D. 100. The *Encyclopedia Britannica*, from a liberal viewpoint, conveys, "Matthew, the first of the four New Testament Gospels, was composed in Greek, probably sometime after A.D. 70, with evident dependence on the *earlier* Gospel according to Mark. There has, however, been extended discussion about the possibility of an *even earlier* version in Aramaic. Numerous textual indications point to an author who was a Jewish Christian writing for Christians of similar background."[24]

While liberal scholars generally date the autographs of the Gospels between A.D. 70 and 100, there is significant internal evidence which, according to conservative scholars, strongly indicates an earlier date. Take, for instance, the biblical Book of Acts. A great portion of the Book of Acts centers on Jerusalem, the temple, Paul's conversion, and Paul's missionary activities. Interestingly, the author does not mention the deaths of three central figures of the book: James, the brother of Jesus (A.D. 62), Peter (A.D. 65–68), and Paul (A.D. 67–68), but does mention the deaths of two minor figures: Stephen and James, the brother of John. The author furthermore fails to mention some major historical events, such as the burning of Rome and the persecution of Christians there (A.D. 64), as well as the destruction of the temple (A.D. 70). The author then ends abruptly with Paul's imprisonment in

Rome (A.D. 63). Why would the author choose to omit such vital information had he been writing after these events had already taken place? Conservative scholars believe the only reasonable explanation (based on this and other historical data) is that the biblical Book of Acts was written no later than A.D. 63.

The Book of Acts is a continuation of the preceding gospel of Luke, which scholars widely agree was the last of the synoptic Gospels to be written.[25] If Acts is given an authorship date of A.D. 63, as suggested above, then all three *preceding* synoptic Gospels must have been in circulation previous to that date. In other words, all three synoptic gospels, which tell the story of the life of Jesus, would have been written before A.D. 63, within about 30 years of Jesus' death in A.D. 30.

William Albright, one of the greatest archaeologists of the 20th century, declared, "We can already say emphatically that there is no longer any solid basis for dating any book of the New Testament after about A.D. 80." He also states, "Every book of the New Testament [excluding Luke who was possibly not Jewish] was written by a baptized Jew between the forties and eighties of the first century A.D."[26] Finally, he asserts, "Only modern scholars who lack both historical method and perspective" could come to a conclusion of much later authorship of the New Testament.[27]

When Was the Gospel First Preached?

Regardless of when the Gospel books were actually written, it is certain, as a fact of history, that the central message of the Gospel (that Jesus had risen from the dead) was being preached almost immediately following Jesus' death in A.D. 30. There are several reasons for this certainty, one of which is the date of Paul's conversion to Christianity.

After first being a bitter enemy of the Christian faith, Paul later became one of the most important figures in its history. When Paul first appeared on the scene of history, he was among the first to participate in serious Christian persecutions. Shortly after, however, he had an experience which convinced him that the Christian message was correct, and that Jesus had in fact risen from the dead. As the *Encyclopedia Britannica* notes, "Converted only a few years after the death of Jesus [Paul's conversion experience] convinced him that Jesus was risen from the dead and exalted as Lord in heaven, as the Christians claimed."[28] During the following years, Paul's life was completely turned around. He went on several large missionary journeys and played a leading role in extending Christianity into a worldwide faith.

Paul's conversion experience as a historical fact is untested by even the most liberal of scholars. The *Encyclopedia Britannica* notes, "Once the basis of Paul's thought in the context of Jewish concepts of his time is understood in the light of modern scholarship . . . Paul stands out more clearly as a Christian Jew, whose conversion experience convinced him that Christ was the universal Lord under God, the agent and leader of God's kingdom."[29]

Historically then, the Christian converts whom Paul first persecuted, before his own conversion to Christianity, are proof that the message of the resurrection of Jesus was already being preached (probably for several years) *before* Paul's conversion, which most scholars date as early as A.D. 35 (just five years after Jesus' death).[30]

To summarize, Paul was at first a bitter enemy of Christianity, and he zealously persecuted any Christian converts he could find. But, scholars agree, about five years following the death of Jesus Christ, Paul himself became converted to Christianity (i.e., he became convinced, somehow, as had the Christians before him, that Jesus had actually risen from the dead). Thus, it is historically certain today that the central message of Christianity, that Jesus had risen from the dead, was being preached *at least* as early as A.D. 35, the acknowledged time of Paul's conversion, within five years of Jesus' death.

Indeed, most scholars agree, the Apostles were at least *preaching* Jesus' resurrection within less than five years of His death. But could there have been any *truth* to such first-century claims?

Footnotes

1 There is now some rising controversy that the scrolls could have a later date of origin than previously thought.

2 The information in this paragraph has been taken almost directly from the "Scrolls from the Dead Sea Exhibition," Library of Congress, 1997, <http://lcweb.loc.gov/exhibits/scrolls/toc.html>

3 "Biblical literature," Encyclopedia Britannica Online, <http://members.eb.com/bol/topic?eu=119705&sctn=18>

4 "The Gospel According to Archaeology," *National Post*, October 23, 1999, p. B6.

5 "Archaeologists Bolster Faith with Round of Biblical Finds," Associated Press, December 15, 1996.

6 "Is the Bible True?" *U.S. News & World Report*, October 25, 1999, cover story.

7 The examples listed are taken from "Archaeologists Bolster Faith with Round of Biblical Finds," Associated Press.

8 "Is the Bible True?" *U.S. News & World Report*.

9 W.F. Albright, *The Archaeology of Palestine and the Bible* (New York, NY: Revell, 1935), p. 127. In matters of biblical scholarship, reference materials such as encyclopedias usually take a liberal viewpoint. Commenting specifically on the Book of Luke, for example, the *Encyclopedia Britannica* states that "historically reliable information cannot be expected [from Luke's Gospel] because his sources were not historical, but were embedded in tradition and proclamation." However, as demonstrated, this type of skepticism has been falsified time and again by continuous archaeological discoveries. With respect to the Gospel of Luke, skeptics have had to admit that archaeology has repeatedly shown the author's writings to be historically reliable, especially his second book, Acts. As respected Oxford historian Sherwin-White wrote, "It is astonishing that while Graeco-Roman historians have been growing in confidence, the 20th century study of the Gospel

narratives, starting from no-less-promising material, has taken so gloomy a turn in the developments of form criticism. . . . For Acts, the confirmation of historicity is overwhelming. . . . Any attempt to reject its basic historicity must now appear absurd." A.N. Sherwin-White, *Roman Society and Roman Law in the New Testament* (Oxford: Clarendon Press, 1963), p. 107, 189.

10 Michael J. Wilkins and J.P. Moreland, editors, *Jesus Under Fire*, (Grand Rapids, MI: Zondervan Publishing House, 1995), p. 221. Furthermore, Gary Habermas has cited a total of 39 ancient extra-biblical sources, including 17 non-Christian, that witness from outside the New Testament to over 100 details of Jesus' life, death, and resurrection. Gary Habermas, *The Verdict of History* (Nashville, TN: T. Nelson, 1988).

11 "Jesus Christ (Non-Christian sources)," Encyclopedia Britannica Online, <http://members.eb.com/bol/topic?eu=109559&sctn=2>

12 "Josephus Flavius," Encyclopedia Britannica Online, <http://members.eb.com/bol/topic?eu=45021&sctn=1>

13 "Testimony of Flavius," *Antiquities*, XVIII, 63ff. This is one of the larger of several passages in Josephus's writings which refers to Jesus. Most scholars agree that this particular passage has an authentic core but also includes later Christian insertions.

14 "Annals of Tacitus," XV, 44; see "Jesus Christ (Non-Christian sources)," Encyclopedia Britannica Online, <http://members.eb.com/bol/topic?eu=109559&sctn=2>

15 "Pliny the Younger," Epistle 10, 96ff; again see "Jesus Christ (Non-Christian sources)," Encyclopedia Britannica Online.

16 "Vita Claudii," 25:4; see "Jesus Christ (Non-Christian sources)," Encyclopedia Britannica Online.

17 "Toledot Yeshua"; see "Jesus Christ (Non-Christian sources)," Encyclopedia Britannica Online.

18 John P. Meier, *A Marginal Jew: Rethinking the Historical Jesus* (New York, NY: Doubleday, 1991), p. 177.

19 This table has been derived from various sources, as follows: F.W. Hall, *Companion to Classical Text*, "MS Authorities for the Text of the Chief Classical Writers" (Oxford: Clarendon Press, 1913), as cited in *Evidence that Demands a Verdict*, Josh McDowell (Nashville, TN: T. Nelson, 1972); also Bruce Manning Metzger, *The Text of the New Testament: Its Transmission, Corruption, and Restoration*, 2nd ed. (New York, NY: Oxford University Press, 1968), p. 36–41; also F.F. Bruce, *The New Testament Documents: Are They Reliable* (Grand Rapids, MI: Eerdmans, 1960), p. 16–17. See also "Biblical Literature,"

Encyclopedia Britannica Online, <http://members.eb.com/bol/topic?idxref=523796>.

20 "Biblical literature," Encyclopedia Britannica Online, <http://members.eb.com/bol/topic?eu=119712&sctn=9>. The earliest known fragment of the New Testament, the *John Ryland Manuscript* located in the John Ryland Library of Manchester, England, dated A.D. 130, was written 40 years or less after the presumed date of the production of that Gospel. Other ancient manuscript copies of the New Testament include the *Chester Beatty Papyri*, containing major portions of the New Testament and dated early 3rd century; the *Bodmer Papyrus*, dated late 2nd century; the *Codex Sinaiticus*, dated A.D. 350; and the *Codex Vaticanus*, dated A.D. 325–350. See two more articles on "Biblical literature" in Encyclopedia Britannica Online, <http://members.eb.com/bol/topic?eu=119712&sctn=15>, and <http://members.eb.com/bol/topic?eu=119712&sctn=13>.

21 Sir Frederic G. Kenyon, *The Bible and Modern Scholarship* (London: J. Murray, 1948), p. 20, as cited in McDowell, *Evidence That Demands A Verdict*.

22 Sir Frederic G. Kenyon, *The Story of the Bible* (London: Murray, 1967), p.133.

23 Sir Frederic G. Kenyon, *Our Bible and the Ancient Manuscripts* (London: Eyre and Spottiswoode, 1941), p. 23, as cited in McDowell, *Evidence That Demands a Verdict*, p. 45.

24 "Gospel of Matthew," Encyclopedia Britannica Online, <http://members.eb.com/bol/topic?eu=52722&sctn=1>. Emphasis added.

25 The majority of New Testament scholarship widely agrees that both Luke and Acts were authored by the same person, and that Acts is a continuation of Luke. ("Acts of the Apostles," Encyclopedia Britannica Online, <http://members.eb.com/bol/topic?eu=3660&sctn=1>)

26 *Christianity Today*, Jan. 18, 1963; also William Albright, *From the Stone Age to Christianity* (Garden City, NY: Doubleday, 1946), p. 23.

27 Albright, *From the Stone Age to Christianity*, p.297–298.

28 "Saint Paul," Encyclopedia Britannica Online, <http://members.eb.com/bol/topic?artcl=108605&seq_nbr=1&page=p&isctn=1> & <http://members.eb.com/bol/topic?artcl=108605&seq_nbr=1&page=n&isctn=2>

29 "Saint Paul," Encyclopedia Britannica Online, <http://members.eb.com/bol/topic?artcl=108605&seq_nbr=1&page=n&isctn=2>

30 See "Saint Paul," Encyclopedia Britannica Online, <http://members.eb.com/bol/topic?artcl=108605&seq_nbr=1&page=p&isctn=1>.

———◦•◦———

Chapter Seven

THE
UNRIVALED
RESURRECTION

*WHAT DO SOME OF
THE WORLD'S GREATEST
LAWYERS SAY ABOUT
THE EVENT THAT
CHANGED HISTORY
FROM B.C. TO A.D.?*

D
r. Simon Greenleaf
was a key founder
of Harvard's School
of Law. He is regarded as one
of the principal figures responsible for Harvard's eminent
position among law schools in
the United States,[1] and he produced possibly the greatest
single authority on evidence in
the entire literature of legal
procedure.[2]

After a challenge by one
of his students to disprove the
claims of Jesus and the Bible,
Greenleaf was certain that a
careful examination of the internal witness of the Gospels
would dispel all the myths at

the heart of Christianity. He determined, once and for all, to expose the myth of the resurrection of Jesus. After thoroughly examining the evidence, however, he came to an extraordinary conclusion.

With a lawyer's skill, Greenleaf put his principles to work as he examined the historical evidence surrounding the resurrection of Jesus Christ as recorded in the ancient writings of the biblical text. After careful study, he wrote *The Testimony of the Evangelists*, in which he stated that it was "impossible that the Apostles could have persisted in affirming the truths they had narrated, had not Jesus Christ actually risen from the dead."

What caused Greenleaf, as one of the most prestigious lawyers of all time, to come to such a dramatic conclusion? In spite of the sensationalist nature of such a suggestion, this chapter briefly examines some of the arguments both for and against the idea that Jesus Christ could have actually risen from the dead two millennia ago.

The alleged bodily resurrection of Jesus, if true, was very consequential concerning mankind's most fearful and important questions. By publicly preaching the Resurrection message in the first century, the Apostles strived to adjust the opinions of mankind upon subjects in which people are not only deeply concerned, but usually stubborn and closed-minded, despite reason or persuasion. Men could not be utterly careless in such a case as this. (As evidenced in ancient writings, two thousand years ago religion and tradition generally played a much more significant role than in today's Western society.) Thus, whoever entertained the account of Jesus, whether Jew or non-Jew, could not have avoided the following reflection: "If these things be true, I must give up the opinions and principles in which I have been brought up, the religion in which my forefathers lived and died." It is not likely that one would do this upon any idle report or trivial account, or indeed without being fully convinced of the truth of that which he or she believed in. But it did not stop at opinions. Those who believed Christianity acted upon it. Many made it the express business of their lives to publicize their new faith. It was required of them to change forthwith their conduct; to take up a different course of life and begin a new set of rules and system of behavior; in doing so they encountered opposition, danger, and persecution."[3]

— William Paley, 1794

The first few hundred years of Christianity were characterized by some of the worst persecution in history.[4] Right from the beginning, the Christian founders were persecuted and eventually put to death for the message they preached: that they had seen Jesus physically risen from the dead.

What, in fact, is it that caused the first followers of Jesus to be willing to die for such a message?

RESURRECTION REASONING

Without a doubt, the most unbelievable aspect of Christianity is in the life of Jesus himself. In His alleged resurrection from the dead, Jesus stands out more remarkably in history than any other human being. It is for this reason that the New Testament, perhaps more than any other book in history, has been subjected to some of the most rigorous historical and literary criticism.

Now, at the beginning of the 21st century, contemporary scholarship has shown that the New Testament firmly stands as the most historically attested work of the ancient world.

All New Testament scholars agree that the Gospels (biographies of Jesus) were written and circulated within Jesus' generation, during the lifetime of the eyewitnesses. In fact, many scholars argue persuasively that some of the Gospels were written as early as the 50s A.D. (within about 30 years of Jesus' death). This is significant because legends and myths usually take root in foreign lands, or centuries after an event. The legend of Santa Claus, for instance, developed centuries after the historical Saint Nicholas lived.[5] Thus, respected Oxford Professor Sherwin-White states that for the Gospels to be myths or legends, the rate of legendary accumulation would have to be "unbelievable" — more generations are needed. He maintains that it would have been without precedent anywhere in history for a myth to have grown up that fast.[6]

In establishing the truthfulness of the New Testament writers as eyewitnesses to the events of their time, several points must be considered.

First, if the writers fabricated the New Testament Gospels, one would expect them to have construed the story in such a way that would have been most advantageous to their cause, rather than include embarrassing details which could defeat their purpose. However, there are plenty such features in the Gospel accounts which could have proved fatal had the narratives been false.[7]

One significant example is the fact that the Gospel writers record *women* as the first witnesses to Jesus' empty tomb, and then to the resurrected Jesus himself. The significance of this cannot be understated. Women were on a very low rung of the social ladder in first-century Palestine,[8] and their testimony was regarded as so worthless that they were not even allowed to serve as legal witnesses in a Jewish court of law.

In that light, it's remarkable that the Gospel writers would record women as the chief witnesses to the empty tomb of Jesus and then also to the risen Jesus himself. Any fabricated story or later legendary account, in order to gain more credibility, would certainly have portrayed *male* disciples (perhaps Peter or John) as the first to discover the tomb and see the risen Jesus. The fact that women, rather than men, are recorded as the first witnesses to the empty tomb is most plausibly explained by the reality that they were, in fact, the discoverers of the tomb.

It is these types of literary characteristics found throughout the New Testament writings that many scholars believe indicate its historical authenticity. Historian Will Durant explains, "Despite the prejudices and theological preconceptions of the [Gospel writers], they record many incidents that mere inventors would have concealed. . . . That a few simple men should in one generation have invented so powerful and appealing a personality, so lofty an ethic, and so inspiring a vision of human brotherhood, would be a miracle far more incredible than any recorded in the Gospels."[9]

The well-known literary genius C.S. Lewis, former literary professor at Cambridge University and fellow of Oxford University, realized that his in-depth knowledge of literature forced him to treat the Gospel record as a trustworthy account: "I was by now too experienced in literary criticism to regard the Gospels as myth."[10]

From its conception in the first century, both Jews and Romans alike were generally opposed to the development of Christianity. The Christian movement outraged the Jewish leaders because the Christians' proclamations undermined many fundamental Jewish teachings. This inevitably led to great conflict between the Jewish leaders and the Christian converts. The heated controversy sometimes became so huge that it caused uproars in the city streets, necessitating the deployment of Roman peace-keeping troops. The Romans, therefore, began hating the Christian movement also, because in less than 40 years it had begun to threaten the peace of the Roman Empire. This is historically certain because ancient non-biblical sources confirm that the Christian movement had spread as far as Rome by A.D. 64 (within 40 years of Jesus' death), when the Christians, who were already hated there, were persecuted and blamed for the burning of the city.[11]

The heart of the Christian message was always that, after being unjustly crucified, God had miraculously raised Jesus from the dead. The first people to begin proclaiming this message were the 12 Apostles (Jesus' first followers), who are the founders of today's Christian church.

Now if the Apostles were lying about Jesus' resurrection, and His body still lay in the tomb, the opponents of Christianity would have easily been able to contradict their claims. To end the growth of Christianity, the opponents would only have needed to produce the body of Jesus, which would have proved that He was never resurrected, but still lay deceased in His tomb. As journalist Frank Morison illustrates, "If the body of Jesus still lay in the tomb, why didn't anyone say so? A cold and dispassionate statement of the real facts, issued by someone in authority, and publicly exhibited, would have been like a bucket of water upon the kindling fire of the Christian heresy. It would have [virtually] destroyed the growing daily stream of new [Christian] converts."[12]

Even if the Apostles *themselves* had believed in the resurrection of Jesus, it is doubtful they would have generated any following so long as the body remained in the tomb. A movement founded on belief in the resurrection of a dead man's extant corpse would have been impossible.

Throughout the early decades of Christianity, it seems the physical vacancy of the tomb was not in doubt by anyone.

Not one historical record from the first or second century is written attacking the factuality of the empty tomb or claiming discovery of the corpse. No one in the first century was saying that the tomb still contained Jesus' body. Events seem to have conspired to place that beyond the reach of argument. The question was always, "What happened to the body?" Incidentally, the corpse of Jesus has never been found.

Thus, it is today widely recognized that the empty tomb of Jesus is a historical fact. The New Testament critic, D.H. van Daalen, points out, "It is extremely difficult to object to the empty tomb on historical grounds; those who deny it do so on the basis of theological or philosophical assumptions."[13] Jacob Kremer, an Austrian scholar who has specialized in the study of the resurrection, also affirms: "By far most scholars hold firmly to the reliability of the biblical statements about the empty tomb."[14] And he lists 28 prominent scholars in support.

It is interesting that the enemies of Christianity did not so much try to contradict the claims of the early Christians regarding Jesus' missing body, as they tried instead to offer other explanations. The Jews first reacted by saying that Jesus' followers (the Apostles) had stolen the corpse and were lying about His resurrection (Matt. 28:13).

However, the Apostles of the first century would have had no possible motive for such actions. Since they were tortured, flogged, imprisoned, beaten, and put to death for their testimony that they had seen the resurrected Jesus, they had nothing to gain and everything to lose by claiming what they did about Him.[15]

Generally, the reliability of eyewitness testimony can be strengthened if it can be shown that the witness has a vested interest in the opposite of what he testifies. One probably would not doubt a child who confessed to a misdeed which would certainly elicit a spanking from the parent. Since the child has a vested interest in the misdeed not occurring, if he admits to it and risks a spanking, then it is reasonable to believe that the child is telling the truth.

Likewise, the first century Apostles would have had a vested interest in the opposite of what they claimed. Far from a spanking, their punishment often resulted in serious persecution. (Scholars agree that serious Christian persecution started almost immediately following Jesus' death.[16]) Thus it seems reasonable that the Apostles at least *believed* they had seen Jesus risen from the dead. It surely wasn't their commitment to a lie, but rather what they believed to be the truth that brought about their martyrdom. Indeed, why would the Apostles want to deceive their own people (the Jews) into believing in a lie when they knew this deception would mean persecution for themselves and hundreds of their believing friends?

According to one of the world's foremost experts on the Resurrection, critical scholars today have thus universally rejected this conspiracy theory that the Apostles had stolen Jesus' corpse and were lying about His resurrection.[17]

On the other hand, could the opposing Jews or Romans themselves have stolen Jesus' body? Highly doubtful, because if any of the opponents of Christianity knew the whereabouts of Jesus' corpse, they would certainly have exposed the whole affair. As already explained, the quickest and surest answer to the proclamation of the resurrection of Jesus would have been simply to produce His corpse. Thus, no one adheres to this theory today.

In the words of one famous journalist, in a historical sense it is the complete failure of anyone to produce the remains of Jesus, or to point to any tomb, official or otherwise, in which the body remained, which ultimately destroys every theory based on the human removal of the body.[18]

However, another theory that has been raised as an alternative explanation to the resurrection of Jesus is that He didn't die on the cross, but merely fainted from exhaustion and loss of blood. He was then taken down and placed alive in the tomb, and after a couple of days, He escaped and convinced the disciples that He had risen from the dead. Today, however, this theory has been entirely given up by scholars: it would be virtually impossible medically for anyone to have survived the severity of torture and crucifixion, much less not to have escaped death by exposure in the tomb. One prominent physician, Dr. Alexander Metherell, who has extensively studied death by crucifixion, explains what is involved:

> Once a person is hanging in the vertical position, crucifixion is essentially an agonizingly slow death by asphyxiation [suffocation]. The reason is that the stresses on the muscles and diaphragm put the chest into the inhaled position; basically, in order to exhale, the individual must push up on his feet so the tension on the muscles would be eased for a moment. In doing so, the nail would tear through the foot, eventually locking up against the tarsal bones. After managing to exhale, the person would then be able to relax down and take another breath in. Again he'd have to push himself up to exhale. . . . This would go on and on until complete exhaustion would take over, and the person wouldn't be able to push up and breathe anymore. . . . As the person slows down his breathing, he goes into what is called respiratory acidosis — the carbon dioxide in the blood is dissolved as carbonic acid, causing the acidity of the blood to increase. This eventually leads to an irregular heartbeat. . . . And then the

victim dies of cardiac arrest. But even before he dies, the hypovolemic shock would cause a sustained rapid heart rate that would have contributed to heart failure, resulting in the collection of fluid in the membrane around the heart, called a pericardial effusion, as well as around the lungs, which is called a pleural effusion. This is significant because the New Testament records that the Roman soldier drove a spear into Jesus' side, apparently through the right lung and into the heart, resulting in the outpouring of blood and water. This flow of blood and water would have actually been the pericardial effusion and the pleural effusion. The New Testament writer would have had no idea why he saw both blood and a clear fluid come out, yet his description is consistent with modern medical knowledge.[19]

If the soldiers wanted to speed up death, they would break the victim's lower leg bones.[20] This would prevent him from pushing up with his legs so he could breathe, and death by asphyxiation would result in a matter of minutes. The *Encyclopedia Britannica* notes, "Death, apparently caused by exhaustion or by heart failure, could be hastened by shattering the legs with an iron club, so that shock and asphyxiation soon ended [the victim's] life."[21] Only after a victim was confirmed dead by the Roman soldiers would the body have been taken down from the cross.

An article in the *Journal of the American Medical Association* discussing the physical death of Jesus concluded, "Clearly, the weight of the historical and medical evidence indicates that Jesus was dead. . . . Interpretations based on the assumption that Jesus did not die on the cross appear to be at odds with modern medical knowledge."[22]

Due to the unanimous rejection by scholars of the preceding theories, what remains are these historical facts: Jesus died on the Cross, and His body, after being placed in the tomb, was not stolen by His friends or His enemies. But this presents the same 2,000-year-old puzzle: What happened to Jesus' body?

The Apostles certainly *believed* in Jesus' resurrection. Indeed, they pinned nearly everything on it. Without this belief, Christianity could never have come into being — the crucifixion would have remained the final tragedy in the life of Jesus. The origin of Christianity hinges on the belief of the earliest disciples that Jesus had risen from the dead. One of the oldest, and "indisputably genuine" New Testament books (1 Corinthians) affirms this. The *Encyclopedia Britannica* notes, "In one of the most significant of all Pauline texts . . . [Paul] reaffirms the reality of Christ's resurrection — doubted or denied by some — as the very foundation of Christian faith."[23]

How does one explain the *origin* of this belief? The most skeptical critic must postulate something that got the Christian movement going. But what was that "something?"

Was a missing body enough in the first century to spark the idea that Jesus had been raised from the dead? The Apostles didn't seem to think so, for not only did they say that Jesus' tomb was empty, they also claimed to have seen Him alive again, after death.

The New Testament writers record that Jesus showed himself alive after His death by many infallible proofs, and was seen by the Apostles for 40 days (Acts 1:3). In one of the oldest New Testament books, written about A.D. 55, Paul the Apostle quotes an old Christian formula which he received and in turn passed on to his converts: "I passed on to you what was most important and what had also been passed on to me: that Christ died for our sins according to the Scriptures, that he was buried, that he was raised from the dead on the third day according to the Scriptures, and that he appeared to Peter, and then to the twelve apostles" (1 Cor. 15:3–5).

Paul probably received this formula from two disciples, Peter and James, during a fact-finding mission in Jerusalem three years after His own conversion to Christianity.[24]

He continues, "After that, Jesus appeared to more than five hundred of His followers at one time, most of whom are still alive, though some have died by now. Then He appeared to James, and later to all the apostles. Last of all, He appeared to me, long after the others" (1 Cor. 15:6–8).

No scholar denies the genuineness of Paul's writing in this text, written within 25 years of Jesus' death. Even the *Encyclopedia Britannica* concedes that this text dates between "20–30 years after Jesus' crucifixion" and is "indisputably genuine."[25] Of crucial significance, then, is that Paul appeals to his audience's knowledge of the fact that Jesus had been seen by more than five hundred people at one time; he reminds them that the majority of these people were still alive and could be questioned.

William Lillie, head of the department of biblical study at the University of Aberdeen, notes the relevance of this fact: "Such a statement in an admittedly genuine letter written within thirty years of the event is almost as strong evidence as one could hope to get for something that happened nearly two thousand years ago. . . . What gives a special authority to the list [of witnesses in Paul's writing] as historical evidence is the reference to most of the five hundred brethren being still alive. St. Paul says in effect, 'If you do not believe me, you can ask them.' "[26]

The first century witnesses to whom Paul referred here could have certainly confirmed or denied the accuracy of his statements about them seeing the resurrected Jesus. Risking persecution, they would have had no reason to lie; there were sometimes mass Christian executions, which began in the first century.[27] If hundreds of these witnesses had denied seeing the post-mortem Jesus, then Paul's credibility would have been utterly destroyed (not to mention the credibility of all the other Apostles as well). Any contrary testimony from the list of these five hundred witnesses would have drastically hindered (if not prevented) the spread of Christianity. But Christianity did not stop. In fact, in the face of persecution, it continued to spread beyond all reasonable expectation. Despite persecution, by about A.D. 70 (only 40 years after Jesus' death), Christianity had spread almost everywhere in the East, from Egypt to the Black Sea, in Bithynia and in Greece, and even as far as Rome.[28]

Exactly what took place with these alleged appearances of Jesus is a subject of scholarly debate. Yet it is widely agreed that *something* did take place, because it is certain that those who claimed to have seen the resurrected Jesus were, in fact, truly convinced that He was risen from the dead. Regarding Paul's own appearance experience, for instance, the *Encyclopedia Britannica* notes, "Though it is impossible to state exactly what happened, the central feature was certainly Paul's vision of Jesus in glory. It convinced him that Jesus was risen from the dead and exalted as Lord in heaven."[29]

Recall that scholars are in agreement that Paul's sudden conversion to Christianity around A.D. 35 is an established historical fact. Since Paul states that his conversion was due to the latest appearance by Jesus, this means that all the previous appearance experiences he refers to must have occurred even earlier, at most within five years of Jesus' death in A.D. 30. It is thus idle to dismiss the accounts of the appearances as mythical; Paul's information makes it historically certain that on separate occasions, within a few years of Jesus' death, various individuals and groups claimed to have seen Jesus alive from the dead. As Norman Perrin, the late New Testament critic of the University of Chicago, notes, "The more we study the tradition with regard to the appearances, the firmer the rock begins to appear upon which they are based."[30] "This conclusion is virtually indisputable," says leading Resurrection expert William Lane Craig.[31]

But while the Resurrection appearances were described in the first century as true appearances of Jesus, today other explanations have been offered.

One suggestion is that the appearances were just hallucinations, or that the Apostles envisioned only a spiritual resurrection. But for a first century Jew, the idea that a man might be raised from the dead spiritually, but not bodily, was simply a contradiction in terms; the Jewish conception of resurrection was always physical. In the words of the much-respected scholar E.E. Ellis: "It is very unlikely that the earliest Palestinian Christians could conceive of any distinction between resurrection and physical, 'grave-emptying' resurrection. To them an anastasis [resurrection] without an empty grave would have been about as meaningful as a square circle."[32] So when the Apostles spoke of Jesus' resurrection, they always mentioned (either explicitly or implicitly) the empty tomb, signifying a physical resurrection.[33]

But could the appearances have simply been hallucinations, from which people mistakenly inferred Jesus' resurrection? This theory became popular during the 19th century and carried over into the first half of the 20th century as well. The problem with this theory, however, is that it is psychologically implausible to postulate such a chain of hallucinations. Scholar William Lane Craig explains that the evidence shows that "Jesus was seen not once, but many times; not by one person, but by several; not only by individuals, but also by groups; not at one locale and circumstance but at many; not by believers only, but by skeptics and unbelievers as well.

The hallucination theory cannot be plausibly stretched to accommodate such diversity."[34]

Typically, hallucinations are projections of one's own mind, and, in a highly emotional state, are triggered by extreme expectation.[35] It is therefore inconceivable that an enemy of Christianity should hallucinate something he opposes, much less transform his life as a consequence: no scholar denies that Paul first appeared on the scene of history as a persecutor of the early church, and later became one of its key proponents.

Additionally, the Gospels state that on several occasions the Apostles did not recognize Jesus. In normal experience, to witness someone alive again after death would, no doubt, cause anyone to question his or her sanity. That is, in fact, what the Gospels record. According to the narratives, none of Jesus' followers expected him to rise from the dead. Luke's Gospel says that when Jesus suddenly appeared to them, "they were terribly frightened, thinking they were seeing a ghost." The gospel relates that Jesus asked, "'Why are you frightened? Why do you doubt who I am? Look at my hands. Look at my feet. You can see that it's really me. Touch me and make sure that I am not a ghost, because ghosts don't have bodies, as you see that I do!' As he spoke, he held out his hands for them to see, and he showed them his feet. Still they stood there doubting, filled with joy and wonder" (Luke 24:37–41).

Renowned Oxford professor C.S. Lewis observed the significance of such an account: "Any theory of hallucination breaks down on the fact that on three separate occasions this hallucination was not immediately recognized as Jesus."[36]

Nor can hallucinations account for the full scope of the evidence. The theory leaves the empty tomb unexplained, and therefore fails as a complete and satisfying explanation.

Thus, like the empty tomb, the first century claims of Jesus' resurrection appearances are left as unexplained historical facts.

In summary, the general consensus of modern scholarship accepts the following ten details as established historical facts:

1. Jesus died by crucifixion 2,000 years ago.
2. Jesus was then placed in a tomb.
3. A few days later, the tomb was found empty.
4. Soon after, the Apostles began testifying that Jesus had risen from the dead.
5. The Apostles really *believed* they had seen Jesus alive again.
6. Even opponents and skeptics of Christianity at the time claimed to have seen Jesus alive again, and their lives were transformed as a consequence.
7. Almost all of the Apostles eventually died for their testimony that they had seen the resurrected Jesus.
8. In the face of brutal persecution, the movement of Christianity grew beyond all reasonable expectation.
9. The belief that Jesus was physically raised from the dead was central and foundational to Christianity from the very beginning.
10. The corpse of Jesus has never been produced.

Every attempt at an alternative explanation to the physical resurrection of Jesus thus far has failed to provide a plausible account for all of the preceding facts, and therefore has been universally rejected by contemporary scholarship.[37]

Yet unquestionably, *something* must have happened two thousand years ago that was so dramatic it changed the course of history from B.C. to A.D.

But as long as liberal and non-liberal scholars alike reject all the preceding theories, how *do* they explain the facts of the empty tomb, the Resurrection appearances, and the origin of the Christian faith? Remarkably, modern scholarship recognizes no plausible naturalistic explanatory theory — liberal scholars are self-confessedly left without an explanation, maintaining there is not enough evidence to reach a firm conclusion.[38]

The official journal of the Society of Humanist Philosophers, *Philo*, an atheistic periodical that "gathers some of the best minds in the world to provide rigorous critiques of religious ideas and doctrines," acknowledges, "We skeptics have definitely not been keeping up our end of the debate in the philosophy of religion. Theistic philosophers have recently written a great deal about the historical arguments for the resurrection of Jesus. These arguments are backed by an impressive degree of historical and biblical scholarship and cannot be lightly dismissed."[39]

Indeed, these three great facts — the empty tomb, the Resurrection appearances, and the origin of the Christian faith — all lead conservative scholars to one conclusion: The bodily resurrection of Jesus.

One basic principle of logic says that simple explanations, rather than complex ones that require many assumptions and complicated reasoning, are most often correct. Extraordinarily then, the resurrection of Jesus would be the simplest explanation for all the facts involved — it requires the least number of assumptions and minimal complex reasoning. Any alternative theory must plausibly account for all the facts of the case, and as yet, scholars recognize none as satisfactory.

Yet there are *philosophical* objections to such a spectacular conclusion. Many people believe that *any* alternative theory, however implausible, is more probable than the idea that God actually raised Jesus from the dead.

One popular approach to exploring events is that which is presented by David Hume. It says that it is acceptable to believe an experience that conforms to normal, ordinary human experiences. Anything that is unique so far as normal human experience is concerned — such as a miracle — should be rejected. For example, which is more probable: that the witnesses of Jesus' resurrection appearances were mistaken, or that God raised Jesus from the dead? According to Hume's point of view the answer is obvious, because miracles simply cannot happen.

But professor Clark Pinnock points out, "The experience against miracles is [consistent] only if we know that all the reports about miracles are false, and this we do not know. No one has an infallible knowledge of 'natural laws', so that he can exclude from the outset the very possibility of unique events. Science can tell us what *has* happened, but it cannot tell us what *may* or *may not* happen. It observes events; it does not create them. The historian does not dictate what history can contain; he is open to whatever the witnesses report. An appeal to Hume bespeaks ignorance of history."[40]

Today the notion that miracles *can* occur does not contradict science or any known facts of experience — it is now widely known that there is actually *no* scientific reason to reject the possibility of a miracle. Today, physicists virtually unanimously agree that time, space, and matter originated together at some finite point in the past. In other words, the universe had a beginning.[41] Thus, most modern scientists agree that it is at least possible that a God (who exists *outside* of the universe) could have created the universe. As famous cosmologist Stephen Hawking remarks, "So long as the universe had a beginning, we could suppose it had a creator."[42] In fact, Hawking suggests, "It would be very difficult to explain why the universe should have begun in just this way, except as the act of a God who intended to create beings like us."[43]

If the possibility of God exists, then so does the possibility of miracles. Thus, the possibility of a miracle cannot, and should not, be ruled out. And thus logically, the possibility that God raised Jesus from the dead also should not be ruled out.

Living in the 21st century, however, many individuals believe that, in order for something to be credible, there must be scientific proof: "If Jesus has risen from the dead, then prove it scientifically!"

Unfortunately, there is a problem with proving anything scientifically about a person or event in history: it is impossible. One must realize that there is a difference between scientific proof and legal-historical proof. The following excerpt illustrates the distinction:

> Scientific proof is based on showing that something is a fact by repeating the event in the presence of the person questioning the fact. There is a controlled environment where observations can be made, data drawn, and hypotheses empirically verified. . . . Testing the truth of a hypothesis by the use of controlled experiments is one of the key techniques of the modern scientific method. For example, somebody says, "Ivory soap doesn't float." So I take the person to the kitchen, put eight inches of water in the sink at 82.7°, and drop in the soap. Plunk. Observations are made, data are drawn, and a hypothesis is empirically verified: Ivory soap floats.
>
> Now if the scientific method was the only method of proving something, you couldn't prove that you went to your first hour class this morning or that you had lunch today. There's no way you can repeat those events in a controlled situation.
>
> To prove an event that has taken place in the past, one must look at legal-historical proof, which is based on showing beyond a reasonable doubt that something is fact. In other words, a verdict is reached

on the basis of the weight of the evidence. That is, there's no reasonable basis for doubting the decision. This kind of proof depends upon three types of testimony: oral testimony, written testimony, and exhibits (such as a gun, bullet, notebook). Using the legal method of determining what happened, you could pretty well prove beyond a reasonable doubt that you were in class this morning: your friends saw you, you have your notes, the professor remembers you.

The scientific method can be used only to prove repeatable things; it isn't adequate for proving or disproving many questions about a person or event in history. The scientific method isn't appropriate for answering questions such as, "Did George Washington live?" "Was Martin Luther King a civil rights leader?" "Who was Jesus of Nazareth?" "Was Robert Kennedy attorney general of the USA?" "Was Jesus Christ raised from the dead?" These are out of the realm of scientific proof, and we need to put them in the realm of legal proof. In other words, the scientific method, which is based on observation, the gathering of data, hypothesizing, deduction, and experimental verification to find and explain empirical regularities in nature, doesn't have the final answers to such questions as, "Can you prove the Resurrection?" or "Can you prove that Jesus is the Son of God?" When men and women rely upon the legal-historical method, they need to check out the reliability of the testimonies.[44]

And that is exactly what Tom Anderson did. As former president of the California Trial Lawyers Association and voted by the *National Law Journal* as one of the top ten trial lawyers in America today, Tom accepted a challenge to "examine history or archaeology or any other discipline" in order to discredit the resurrection of Jesus. In his words: "My four month study was motivated to find a loophole, any loophole, in the truths of Christ. Finding none frightened me."[45]

Ultimately, given the things Jesus said, it must logically follow that He was either a liar, a lunatic, or truly God — for the New Testament records the following about Jesus: He claimed that God was His Father, and He claimed to be one with His Father (Matt. 11:27; John 5:16–18; John 10:30). He claimed to be the *I AM* ("I AM" is a name for God in the Old Testament; see John 8:51–58; Exod. 3:14). He claimed to come forth from God (John 3:13, 8:23, 42). He claimed to be the only access to God, His Father (John 14:6–7). He claimed to be able to forgive sins (Matt. 9:2–7). He claimed to be the judge of all mankind and to dishonor Him was to dishonor God His Father (John 5:22–23). He claimed to have had glory with His Father before the world began (John 17:5). He accepted worship (Matt. 14:33; John 20:28–29). The authenticity of these sayings of Jesus is quite certain, as they would have proved fatal to any fabrication or myth: most of these sayings are blasphemous to Jewish tradition today, and would have been also in the first century. Since the Apostles were trying to convince the Jews that Jesus was the prophesied Savior (or Messiah) of the Old Testament, it would have been impossible to make their case by attributing to Him such blasphemy. Indeed, the Gospels show that it was precisely these "blasphemous" claims that infuriated the Jewish leaders (John 8:58–59; Matt. 9:2–3), ultimately resulting in Jesus' crucifixion.

Thus, Jesus was either telling the truth or not, as the following flowchart illustrates:

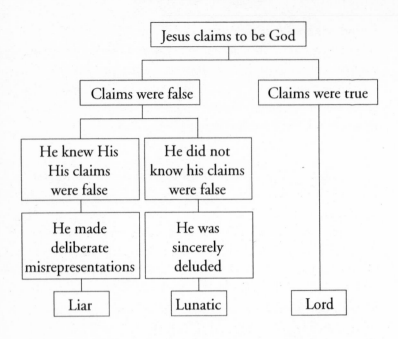

The issue with these three alternatives is not which is possible, for it is obvious that all three are possible. Rather, the question is, "Which is more probable?" To conclude logically that Jesus was a liar or lunatic, however, doesn't coincide with what is known either of Him or the results of His life and teachings. Everything about Jesus' life indicates that He is a perfect model of sanity and decency. Indeed, scholars, non-Christians, and even atheists throughout history have acknowledged the moral superiority of Jesus. As the world-renowned Canadian agnostic Charles Templeton states, "Jesus was a moral genius. He was the intrinsically wisest person that I've ever encountered in my life or in my readings. . . . There's no question that He had the highest moral standard, the least duplicity, and the greatest compassion of any human being in history."[46]

There are yet two more factors that must also be accounted for: (1) some people have claimed to be God, but most have not; and (2) some people are regarded as sages (i.e., they possessed great wisdom), but most are not. These points seem strange, but their significance is clarified in the following four possible combinations: (1) There are those who have not claimed to be God and are not regarded as sages — this accounts for most people who have ever lived; (2) There are those who have not claimed to be God but are regarded as sages — examples would be people such as Moses, Socrates, and Plato; (3) There are those who have claimed to be God but are not regarded as sages. These people have generally been regarded as insane — David Koresh would be an example; (4) There are those who have claimed to be God and are regarded as sages. Only one person in history fits this category — Jesus Christ. Thus, Jesus imposes himself upon mankind and forces each person to a decision about who he or she thinks He is. (See chart below.)

		Claimed to Be God	
		No	Yes
Regarded as Sage	No	Most People	Insane
	Yes	Moses Socrates, Plato	Jesus

In the end, the latest critical attempts to undermine the traditional, literal interpretation of the Gospels have been shown to be highly unfounded. Although gaining popularity in the media, radical New Testament critics have unfortunately misconstrued the facts surrounding the historical resurrection of Jesus. Conservative and even many liberal scholars today have been able to show that the latest historical and archaeological research tends only to strengthen the conclusions of some of history's greatest lawyers.

Concluded Tom Anderson, former president of the California Trial Lawyers Association and one of today's top ten trial lawyers, "You see, my four-month study was motivated to find a loophole, any loophole, in the truths of Christ. Finding none frightened me."[47] Similarly, Simon Greenleaf, who produced possibly the greatest single authority on evidence in the entire literature of legal procedure, concluded that it is "impossible that the Apostles could have persisted in affirming the truths they had narrated, had not Jesus Christ actually risen from the dead."[48] And Sir Lionel Luckhoo, whose 245 consecutive murder trial victories earned him a place in The Guinness Book of World Records as the world's most successful lawyer,[49] concluded that "the evidence for the resurrection of Jesus Christ is so overwhelming that it compels acceptance by proof which leaves absolutely no room for doubt."[50]

Footnotes

1 See "Simon Greenleaf," A&E's Biography.com, <http://www.biography.com>

2 *Dictionary of American Biography*, Vol. 4 (New York, NY: Charles Scribner's Sons, 1928–1936).

3 Excerpt derived from an essay in *A View of the Evidences of Christianity*, William Paley (Philadelphia, PA: Thomas Dobson, 1794).

4 For example, see "Diocletian," Encyclopedia Britannica Online, <http://members.eb.com/bol/topic?artcl=30521&seq_nbr=1&page=p&isctn=4>.

5 "Saint Nicholas," Encyclopedia Britannica Online, <http://members.eb.com/bol/topic?xref=11608>

6 A.N. Sherwin-White, *Roman Society and Roman Law in the New Testament* (Oxford: Clarendon Press, 1963), p. 107.

The idea that the New Testament writers borrowed important beliefs and practices from a number of ancient pagan mystery religions, though still propagated by some philosophers and educators, has been virtually entirely given up today by informed New Testament scholars for many reasons. (For a detailed discussion, see the article *Was the New Testament Influenced by Pagan Religions?* by Ronald Nash, *Christian Research Journal*, Winter 1994, <http://www.equip.org/free/DB109.htm>.) Note that, whatever the case, the New Testament account of the death and resurrection of a human being as an actual historical event at a particular point and place in history has absolutely no parallel in any pagan religion or cult.

7 For instance, the writers record numerous statements about Jesus' words and life that are difficult to explain, and initially appear counterproductive to the purpose of the story. Some examples include Jesus' seeming denial of being good (Mark 10:18), His display of anger (Matt. 21:12), and the unbelief of His own family (John 7:5).

8 This is evident in such rabbinic expressions as "Sooner let the words of the law be burnt than delivered to women" and "Happy is he whose children are male, but woe to him whose children are female."

9 Will Durant, *The Story of Civilization*, "Caesar and Christ," Vol. 3 (New York, NY: Simon and Schuster, 1944).

10 C.S. Lewis, *Surprised by Joy* (London: G. Blis, 1955).

11 See "Non-Christian Sources," Encyclopedia Britannica Online, <http://members.eb.com/bol/topic?eu=109559&sctn=2>.

12 Frank Morison, *Who Moved the Stone?* (New York, NY: Barnes & Noble, 1958), p. 116.

13 D.H. Van Daalen, *The Real Resurrection* (London: Collins, 1972), p. 41.

14 Jacob Kremer, *Die Osterevangelien — Geschichten um Geschichte* (Stuttgart: Verlag Katholisches Bibelwerk, 1977), p. 49–50.

15 A combination of biblical and non-biblical historical sources say that almost all of the Apostles became Christian martyrs, while only a few conflicting accounts say that some of the Apostles died naturally. Scholars are generally in agreement, therefore, that as a historical fact most of the Apostles did become martyrs. More information on this topic can be found in the *Encyclopedia Britannica*. For a sample, see "Martyr," Encyclopedia Britannica Online, <http://members.eb.com/bol/topic?eu=52459&sctn=2>

16 The *Encyclopedia Britannica* acknowledges that "serious persecution of Christians first arose" before Paul's conversion, which dates to only a few years after Jesus' death. ("Saint Paul," Encyclopedia Britannica Online, <http://members.eb.com/bol/topic?artcl=108605&seq_nbr=1&page=n&isctn=2>)

17 "Contemporary Scholarship and the Historical Evidence for the Resurrection of Jesus Christ," article by William Lane Craig, <http://www.leaderu.com/truth/1truth22.html>

18 Morison, *Who Moved the Stone?*

19 Lee Strobel, *The Case for Christ* (Grand Rapids, MI: Zondervan, 1998).

20 Archaeological discoveries have corroborated this procedure.

21 "Crucifixion," Encyclopedia Britannica Online, <http://members.eb.com/bol/topic?eu=28494&sctn=1>

22 "On the Physical Death of Jesus Christ," *Journal of the American Medical Association*, March 21, 1986. Furthermore, D.F. Strauss noted long ago, "It is impossible that a being who had stolen half-dead out of the sepulchre, who crept about weak and ill, wanting medical treatment, who required bandaging, strengthening, and indulgence, and who still at last yielded to his sufferings, could have given to the disciples the impression that he was a conqueror over death and the grave, the Prince of Life: an impression which lay at the bottom of their future ministry." David Friedrich Strauss, *New Life of Jesus* (London: Edinburgh, Williams and Norgate, 1865).

23 "Corinthians," Encyclopedia Britannica Online, <http://members.eb.com/bol/topic?eu=26726&sctn=1>

24 "Saint Paul," Encyclopedia Britannica Online, <http://members.eb.com/bol/topic?artcl=108605&seq_nbr=1&page=n&isctn=2>.

25 "Pauline letters," Encyclopedia Britannica Online, <http://members.eb.com/bol/topic?eu=119715&sctn=1>; also "Saint Paul," Encyclopedia Britannica Online, <http://members.eb.com/bol/topic?artcl=108605&seq_nbr=1&page=n&isctn=2>

26 D.E. Nineham et al., *Historicity and Chronology in the New Testament*, "The Empty Tomb and the Resurrection," (London: SPCK, 1965), p. 125.

27 See "Martyr," Encyclopedia Britannica Online, <http://members.eb.com/bol/topic?eu=52459&sctn=2>.

28 "Ancient Rome," Encyclopedia Britannica Online, <http://members.eb.com/bol/topic?eu=109199&sctn=6>. Although the movement "spread with relative slowness" in the first and second centuries, in the face of persecution its growth rate was surprisingly high for so revolutionary a doctrine.

29 Moreover, as discussed earlier, the fact that the first appearances of Jesus were not to the Apostles, but instead to women, tends to indicate further authenticity that the alleged appearances were real events of some kind. As C.F.D. Moule comments, "It is difficult to explain how a story that grew up late and took shape merely in accord with the supposed demands of apologetic came to be framed in terms almost exclusively of women witnesses, who, as such, were notoriously invalid witnesses according to Jewish principles of evidence." C.F.D. Moule, editor, *The Significance of the Message of the Resurrection for Faith in Jesus Christ* (London: S.C.M. Press, 1968), p. 9.

30 Norman Perrin, *The Resurrection According to Matthew, Mark, and Luke* (Philadelphia, PA: Fortress Press, 1974), p. 80.

31 "Contemporary Scholarship and the Historical Evidence for the Resurrection of Jesus Christ," article by William Lane Craig, <http://www.leaderu.com/truth/1truth22.html>

32 E. Earle Ellis, *The Gospel of Luke* (London: Nelson, 1966), p. 273.

33 For a deeper discussion of this, see Craig, "Contemporary Scholarship and the Historical Evidence for the Resurrection of Jesus Christ."

34 Ibid.

35 "Hallucination," Encyclopedia Britannica Online, <http://members.eb.com/bol/topic?eu=119400&sctn=11>

36 C.S. Lewis, *Miracles: A Preliminary Study* (New York, NY: Macmillan Co., 1947). Incidentally, it should also be noted that, as is the case with the women witnesses, had these narratives (of the Apostles' failure to recognize Jesus) been fabricated or mythological, it is unlikely the writers would have included them, since such embarrassing statements would probably pose grave difficulties to the rise of Christianity.

37 Craig, "Contemporary Scholarship and the Historical Evidence for the Resurrection of Jesus Christ."

38 Ibid.

39 Keith M. Parsons, "Uncovering the Other Side of the Debate," *Philo*, vol. 2, no. 1, <http://secularhumanism.org/library/philo/parsons_2_1.html>

40 Clark Pinnock, "The Tombstone That Trembled," *Christianity Today*, April 12, 1968, p. 8 .

41 See Stephen Hawking, *The Illustrated A Brief History of Time* (New York, NY: Bantam Books, 1996), p. 67. Note: In Hawking's alternative "no boundary" proposal (which is a highly controversial model rejected even by some of Hawking's own colleagues, namely Roger Penrose), the notion that the universe has neither beginning nor end is something that exists in mathematical terms only using imaginary numbers and does not correspond to reality, as Hawking himself admits: "Only if we could picture the universe in terms of imaginary time would there be no [beginning]. . . . When one goes back to the real time in which we live, however . . . the universe has a beginning" (p. 179). Hawking confesses, "I don't demand that a theory correspond to reality because I don't know what it is. . . . I take the positivist viewpoint that a physical theory is just a mathematical model and that it is meaningless to ask whether it corresponds to reality." But he does acknowledge that even according to his model, the universe, in fact, *did begin* to exist, though he attributes its existence to absolute nothingness: "[The universe] would quite literally be created out of

nothing: not just out of the vacuum, but out of absolutely nothing at all, because there is nothing outside the universe." Stephen Hawking and Roger Penrose, *The Nature of Space and Time* (Princeton, NJ: Princeton University Press, 1996), p. 121; 3-4; 85. For a brief treatment of Hawking's no boundary proposal, see Craig, "The Ultimate Question of Origins," <http://www.leaderu.com/offices/billcraig/docs/ultimatequestion.html#text47>

42 Hawking, *The Illustrated A Brief History of Time*, p. 181.

43 Ibid., p. 163.

44 This excerpt is derived from Bill Wilson, *The Best of Josh McDowell* (Nashville, TN: T. Nelson, 1993).

45 Tom Anderson, *And the Truth Shall Set You Free*, independent publication; <http://www.anderson-law-firm.com/tta/tta-index.htm>.

46 Lee Strobel, *The Case for Faith* (Grand Rapids, MI: Zondervan Publishing House, 2000).

47 Anderson, *And the Truth Shall Set You Free*.

48 Simon Greenleaf, *The Testimony of the Evangelists* (Grand Rapids, MI: Kregel Publications, 1995). Originally published: New York, NY: J.C. & Co., 1874.

49 *The Guinness Book of World Records*, 1991 edition (New York, NY: Facts on File, 1991), p. 547.

50 Strobel, *The Case for Christ*.

   For a far deeper analysis of the life, death, and resurrection of Jesus, see Michael J. Wilkins and J.P. Moreland, general editors, *Jesus Under Fire* (Grand Rapids, MI: Zondervan Publishing House, 1995).

CONCLUSION

The answer to the question of the origin of the universe has been sought after for many thousands of years. Ancient paganism suggested that the Sun God was somehow responsible. Later religions attributed the creation of the universe to a Supreme Being outside of the universe. Today, many of us think that science can explain it all, eliminating the need for a belief in God.

But no explanation can be without philosophical and religious overtones. Modern physics says that the universe in which we live originated, or began to exist, at some finite point in the past,[1] yet the cause of its origin is completely unknown to science. Cosmologists are still asking the questions: Is our universe all that there is, just the lucky result of a single spontaneous explosion? Or is ours only one of many parallel universes, and just by chance one that happens to be life-permitting? Or even more daring, is our universe the handiwork of an expert Creator, intended exclusively for the existence of life on earth, showing remarkable craftsmanship and design?

If our universe was purposefully designed by a God, we would expect it to be filled with evidence of design as opposed to randomness and disorder. After decades of research and scientific exploration, that is precisely what is being found.

A growing number of scientists are beginning to view the "co-incidences" of the "anthropic principle" as extraordinary "evidence to support the argument that the universe has been designed for our benefit — tailor-made for man." Indeed, despite the public's general unawareness, the idea that a God created this finely tuned universe seems perfectly consistent with what we do observe in the cosmos. However, "most scientists prefer to shy away from the religious side of it," as Stephen Hawking expresses.

With the success of scientific theories in describing things, most people have come to believe that the idea of God is ultimately unnecessary to explain natural phenomena. In other words, the notion of a supernatural Creator is less necessary today because we are now more knowledgeable in the ways of science.

But the problem with this type of reasoning is that, in reality, just the opposite seems true: as science progresses, so does the appearance of design in nature; the more we learn from science, the more complicated we realize nature is. What was once thought to be simple, such as a simple cell, is now known to be more complex than even the most advanced piece of machinery yet created by mankind.

So as we increasingly understand how nature works, we also increasingly realize the depth of complexity and the appearance of design in nature. In effect, the more we progress in science, the less likely it seems that the universe is the product of a mere accident, and therefore the stronger the evidence seems to become for the involvement of a Master Designer. Thus, rather than diminishing the idea that the universe was intentionally designed by a God, the continual progression of science seems to strengthen such a notion.

Most people have also come to think of the theory of evolution as the only scientific explanation for the origin of life. Anyone who resists the theory, it is said, lacks complete understanding of its evidence. But science does have its limits. Many people confuse *origins-science* with the type of science that has sent man to the moon and cured diseases. Yet the operational science that put man on the moon deals only with repeatable, testable experimentation and observation. In contrast, the kind of science that deals with the past, *origins science*, is *not* based on repeatable processes, but is based upon unrepeatable past events.

Since the theory of evolution is supposed to be a story about how life began, this means that it is based upon past events and therefore falls into the category of origins science. Thus, if a person rejects evolution, which deals with *unrepeatable* processes, he or she is *not* rejecting the type of science that put man on the moon.

Nonetheless, there will always be those who persist in making such claims, like the leading evolutionist and self-confessed atheist Stephen Jay Gould, who called creation "unscientific" and "purely religious," and asserted that "biology without evolution is like chemistry without the periodic table."[2]

Of course, many scientists strongly disagree with such charges. A growing number of scientists (including non-creationists) have begun to seriously question the validity of the theory of evolution. In fact, one of the most distinguished of scientists, who also happened to be one of the most knowledgeable zoologists in the world, even went so far as to say that evolution "proves to be in conflict with reality."[3]

So where does all the controversy come from? Surely not from the facts alone, because everyone has the same facts — the same earth, the same fossil layers, the same animals and plants, the same genetic mutations — the facts are all the same. Rather, the controversy arises in the way we all interpret the facts. And why do we interpret facts differently? Because we start with different biases and presuppositions.[4] Indeed, even renowned evolutionist Stephen Jay Gould has admitted on many occasions that it is how we interpret the facts, and what we say they mean about the history of life, that is obviously subject to biased ways of thinking. Thus, when creationists and evolutionists argue about the evidence, in reality they are each arguing about their interpretations based on their presuppositions. The same is also true when evolutionists argue amongst themselves (a regular occurrence).

Perhaps that might help explain these surprising remarks made in 1981 by Colin Patterson, the senior paleontologist from the British Museum of Natural History: "One of the reasons I started taking this anti-evolutionary view was . . . it struck me that I had been working on this stuff for 20 years and there was not one thing I knew about it. That's quite a shock to learn that one can be so misled so long. . . . So for the last few weeks I've tried putting a simple question to various people and groups of people. Question is: Can you tell me anything you know about evolution, any one thing that is true? I tried that question on the geology staff at the Field Museum of Natural History and the only answer I got was silence. I tried it on the members of the Evolutionary Morphology Seminar in the University of Chicago, a very prestigious body of evolutionists, and all I got there was silence for a long time and eventually one person said, 'I do know one thing — it ought not to be taught in high school.' "[5]

Today there are many specific criticisms of evolution that show some of its fundamental assumptions to be unsubstantiated. Probably the most significant criticism (despite evolutionists' desperate attempts to the contrary) is the total failure of anyone to point to any example in which a mutation has actually improved the DNA code by adding new genetic information. Without any evidence that information can arise just by itself, from nothing, there is no indication that evolution is even scientifically possible.[6]

The theory of evolution is heavily based on the assumption that genetic mutations (accidental copying mistakes) can improve an organism's genetic code (i.e., that mutations can create new genetic information). But a random mutation is not likely to improve an organism's genetic code any more than firing a gunshot blindly through the hood of a car is likely to improve engine performance.

Indeed, all of our real-world experience would indicate that to rely on accidental copying mistakes to generate the information required to create complex structures like wings and eyes is the stuff of wishful thinking, not science.

However, because creatures can adapt to changing environments, evolutionists use such changes to show "evolution happening." Yet these types of changes do not support evolution — they are either genetically neutral or genetically downhill, being losses of information instead of the required gains. Losing bits of genetic information a little at a time does not explain how the genetic code was built in the first place; you can't build a business by losing a little bit of money at a time.

Since we never observe an addition of new genetic information when a creature adapts to its environment, but always a shift or loss of already-existing information (genes), it is reasonable to believe that a Creator pre-programmed creatures with enough genetic potential to adapt to future environmental changes.

And despite popular belief, there is not one location on earth where the fossil record shows "a clear vector of progress" as dogmatically proposed in textbooks. In fact, the fossil record seems to fit the creation model well — it is characterized by abrupt appearances of fully formed organisms, with large systematic gaps (lacking transitional forms) between different types of creatures.

If the fossil record offers little support for the theory of evolution (with only a handful of disputed transitional forms), and if virtually all of the observed examples that allegedly show evolution happening do not really support evolution at all (i.e., no example shows an addition of new genetic information, which is required to support the idea that a simple cell could have evolved into a human being) — if these two points are true — then what compelling reason is there to believe in evolution as the sole explanation for our origins, other than out of philosophical necessity?

And though the majority of scientists accept the theory of evolution as true today, should not we be reminded that the majority of scientists also once thought the sun revolved around the earth?

Incidentally, the "biblical scenario for the creation of life turns out to be not far off the mark." It has been demonstrated that the biblical creation model is *not unreasonable* to believe as a fact of history. The creation model stands up to an objective analysis: not only is it reasonable, it is also consistent with what is observed around the earth today (i.e., it can satisfactorily explain things such as fossils and dinosaurs). As such, the biblical Book of Genesis does not need to be looked at as just a "story" — there is good evidence to warrant a literal interpretation of the events narrated.

But not only do creationist scientists argue that the biblical creation model is scientifically sound, they also argue that living things are ordered in such a way as to exhibit evidence of intelligent design. The high information content in the DNA of living things, equivalent to millions of pages of the *Encyclopedia Britannica*, indicates that rather than a random, purposeless evolvement, an intelligent source was ultimately necessary.

In the Search for Extra-Terrestrial Intelligence (SETI), the discovery of a radio signal from outer space with a high level of specified complexity would be hailed as evidence for an intelligent source. So why shouldn't the discovery of high specified complexity in the DNA of living things, equivalent to millions of pages of *Encyclopedia Britannica*, also be hailed as evidence for an intelligent source?

Some of the world's most distinguished scientists, such as Nobel Prize winner Dr. Francis Crick who made possibly the most important discovery of 20th century biology, have thus come to the conclusion that life could never have developed without the aid of a Master Designer.

But others, because of their presuppositions, refuse to come to such conclusions despite the weight of the evidence. One of today's leading evolutionary biologists clearly expresses this dominant mindset:

> It is not that the methods and institutions of science somehow compel us to accept a material [naturalistic] explanation of the . . . world, but, on the contrary . . . we are forced by our [presuppositions] . . . to produce material explanations . . . for we cannot allow a Divine Foot in the door.[7]

But if science is a search for the truth *no matter what the truth might be*, then shouldn't the door remain open to whatever truth is there to be revealed?

———◆———

Even if a Master Designer (God) did create the universe and life on earth, how can we possibly know who this God is? The world's religions are sometimes worlds apart in their description of the nature of God, and they each make varying and contrasting claims regarding many other issues as well. Where one religion says that Jesus is still dead, for instance, another religion says that He has risen from the dead. Such contradictions between various religions and belief-systems mean that not all religions can be true at once.[8] Jesus cannot be both dead and alive at the same time. So how are we to ever find the truth in such a blizzard of conflicting claims?

To determine the tenability of any one particular religion or belief-system, we must test it in areas that it *can* be tested in. We must examine its claims concerning matters of history and science. Suppose some of these claims failed to withstand objective scrutiny; suppose they proved to be false or contradicted other known facts — this would tend to lessen the credibility of a particular belief-system. On the other hand, suppose these claims were instead corroborated by history and archaeology and other such disciplines; suppose they successfully withstood objective scrutiny — this would tend to strengthen the authority and credibility of the religion.

In this way, the Bible holds its ground. The Bible is indeed surprising in some of its scientific accuracy and detail. Some biblical statements even appear to reveal an exceptional knowledge of scientific matters. Under close examination, the Bible has not been seen to make any false scientific statements.

Often the Bible is accused of containing so many obvious discrepancies that it would be foolish to trust it. Yet, while certain passages may at first appear contradictory (as can the testimonies of any two honest witnesses in one legal trial), further investigation commonly shows otherwise.

In fact, the excessive skepticism shown toward the Bible by certain schools of thought has been progressively discredited. Concerning matters of history, for instance, discovery after discovery has established the accuracy of numerous details. Archaeologists are increasingly discovering that their finds are affirming the historical accuracy of the Bible, corroborating key portions of events.

Unlike the various accounts of many mystic religions, the Bible's New Testament narratives describe Jesus as a man of flesh and blood who traveled to actual geographic locations and interacted with known historical persons. In itself, the historicity of Jesus has been firmly established by scholars as an indisputable fact.

Likewise, compared with other ancient documents, the New Testament is unprecedented in its historicity. Concedes the *Encyclopedia Britannica*, "Compared with other ancient manuscripts, the text of the New Testament is dependable and consistent." In fact, when it comes to checking and cross checking the readings of the New Testament, it stands as the most historically attested work of the ancient world.

All New Testament scholars agree that, contrary to popular belief, the New Testament Gospels (the biographies of Jesus) were written and circulated within Jesus' generation, during the lifetime of His contemporaries; many scholars argue persuasively that some of the Gospels were written as early as the 50s A.D. From the time of Jesus' death in A.D. 30, this eliminates any significant time for legend to have accumulated — it would be without precedent anywhere in history for a myth to have grown up that fast.

There is no doubt today among scholars[9] that all of the relevant historical facts surrounding the death and resurrection of Jesus are true; what is in question is how to explain them. If someone reaches the verdict that Jesus did not rise from the dead, then that is fair enough. But they must offer an alternative explanation that is plausible given all of the facts.

However, to date, every alternative explanation to the resurrection of Jesus has failed to provide a plausible account of all the facts of the case, and therefore have all been universally rejected by contemporary scholarship.

To conclude that Jesus did not rise from the dead by maintaining there is not enough evidence to reach a firm conclusion is at odds with the pattern of archaeological discovery during the last century. If the past teaches us anything, it is surely that whenever the evidence from archaeology is unmistakable, it tends always to reinforce the accuracy of the events recorded in the New Testament. The excessive skepticism shown toward the New Testament events has been progressively discredited. More and more, archaeological finds are affirming the historical accuracy of the Bible. It is thus inconsistent to presume that some future discovery will provide a plausible alternative explanation to the resurrection of Jesus — archaeology has repeatedly shown just the opposite.

Today, the simplest and *only* known explanation that can flawlessly explain every relevant fact is that Jesus, like it or not, really did physically rise from the dead. Extraordinarily, there is no historical or scientific[10] reason to reject this conclusion.

As a result, many of the world's greatest lawyers, after studying the subject (including those who had initially set out to *disprove* it), have come to the remarkable conclusion that the resurrection of Jesus is a genuine historical fact.

We are left in the end with the following seven tremendous facts:

1. The calculated odds against the universe forming by chance would, in our everyday experience, normally indicate that it would be impossible.
2. The calculated odds against life forming by chance would, in our everyday experience, normally indicate that it would be impossible.
3. The calculated odds against genetic mutations improving the DNA code would, in our everyday experience, normally indicate that it would be impossible.[11]
4. The DNA code contains meaningful information; yet information never arises without an intelligent source.
5. In explaining the events that transpired after Jesus' death, all alternative explanations to the resurrection of Jesus

have been unanimously rejected by scholars as implausible and or incoherent.

6. The actual physical resurrection of Jesus is really the only known explanation that can flawlessly explain every relevant historical fact of the case.

7. Jesus is the only person in history who is widely regarded as a sage despite His claims to be God.

We may argue that in a rare occurrence, in spite of the vanishingly small odds, both the universe and living things *might* have spontaneously formed by chance, and subsequently evolved. We may also argue that in a rare occurrence, an intelligent source *might not* have been necessary to produce the information contained in the DNA of living things, despite the fact that our everyday experience reveals exactly the opposite. Likewise, we may further argue that some future discovery *might* provide a plausible alternative explanation to the resurrection of Jesus, despite the contrary pattern of archaeological discovery. The problem is, however, that to argue this way is no longer to do science. As physical chemist Dr. Charles Thaxton so clearly points out, "Regular experience, not negligible probabilities and remote possibilities, is the basis of science."[12]

So what shall we conclude from all of this? Despite each of our personal beliefs and presuppositions, if indeed there is a God, and if indeed Jesus truly rose from the dead and is who He claimed to be, then are not His words relevant to each of us today?

> If you don't even believe me when I tell you about things that happen here on earth, how can you possibly believe if I tell you what is going on in heaven? For only I . . . have come to earth and will return to heaven again. . . . For God so loved the world

that he gave his only Son, so that everyone who believes in him will not perish but have eternal life. God did not send his Son into the world to condemn it, but to save it. There is no judgment awaiting those who trust him. But those who do not trust him have already been judged for not believing in the only Son of God (John 3:12–18; NLT).

Here I am! I stand at the door and knock. If anyone hears my voice and opens the door, I will come in and eat with him, and he with me (Rev. 3:20; NIV).

For my purpose is to give life in all its fullness (John 10:10; NLT).

Footnotes

1 Even Stephen Hawking acknowledges the beginning of the existence of the universe, regardless of his proposal of a timeless universe using imaginary time. See Stephen Hawking, *The Illustrated A Brief History of Time* (New York, NY: Bantam Books, 1996).

2 See Stephen Jay Gould, "Dorothy, It's Really Oz," *Time*, vol. 154, no. 8, August 23, 1999.

3 P. Grassé, *Evolution du Vivant* ((New York, NY: Academic Press, 1977)).

4 Many proponents of evolution subscribe to a set of naturalistic and mechanistic — if not atheistic — presuppositions, which disqualifies them from any claim to objectivity in examining matters concerning origins and science.

5 Dr. Colin Patterson, keynote address at the American Museum of Natural History, New York City, New York, November 5, 1981.

6 That is, until a mutation has been observed to improve the DNA code by producing new meaningful information (or instructions), there is no proof that any mechanism (mutations or otherwise) can account for the evolution of living things.

7 Richard Lewontin, "Billions and Billions of Demons," *New York Review,* January 9, 1997, p. 31. This quote typifies the self-confessed atheistic motivation of many leaders today in the scientific community.

8 However, there may be certain "truths" that can be extracted from several religions at once.

9 Except those such as the fellows of the *Jesus Seminar*, whose work is so erroneous it has been progressively discredited even by liberal non-Christian scholars — see Michael J. Wilkins and J.P. Moreland, general editors, *Jesus Under Fire* (Grand Rapids, MI: Zondervan Publishing House, 1995).

10 There is no reason scientifically because the possibility of a miracle does not contradict science or any known facts of experience.

11 A random mutation is not likely to improve an organism's genetic code any more than firing a gunshot blindly through the hood of a car is likely to improve engine performance. – University biology textbook

12 "DNA, Design, and the Origin of Life," article by Charles B. Thaxton, <http://www.leaderu.com/science/thaxton_dna.html>

INDEX

NOTES

_____

_____

_____

_____

_____

_____

_____

_____

_____

_____

_____

_____

_____

_____

_____

_____

_____

_____

_____

_____

_____

_____

NOTES

_____

_____

_____

_____

_____

_____

_____

_____

_____

_____

_____

_____

_____

_____

_____

_____

_____

_____

_____

_____

_____

NOTES

_____

_____

_____

_____

_____

_____

_____

_____

_____

_____

_____

_____

_____

_____

_____

_____

_____

_____

_____

_____

_____

_____

_____